FRUGAL RAW!

RAW on the CHEAP
At Its Finest!

~ Mattye Lee Thompson

FRUGAL RAW!

Mattye Lee Thompson
February 20, 2008

Dedicated to all of my Raw Angels.
To those who have believed in and supported me in this endeavor
and in staying my raw path.
Your motivation and inspiration are my wellspring.

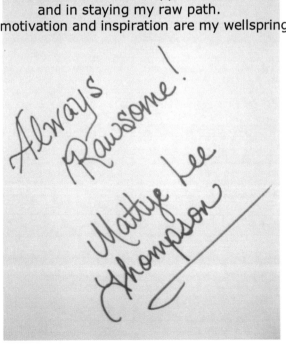

Always
Rawsome!

Mattye Lee
Thompson

TABLE OF CONTENTS

TABLE OF CONTENTS

- Smoothies

- Soups

- Creamy Tomato Soup...75
  - Creamy Avo-Spinach Soup...76

- Appetizers

  - Cheeze Sticks w/Marinara Sauce...78
  - Dolmas...80
  - Raw Falafel w/Tzatziki Sauce...81
  - Herbed Cheeze Stuffed Mushrooms...83
  - Nori Rolls...84

- Cheezes/Pates

  - Garlicky Cashew Cheeze...86
  - Raw "Refried" Beans...87
  - Sunny Eggless Salad...88
  - Cashew Pate Stuffed Tomatoes...89
  - Raw Parm...90
  - Sunny Cream Cheeze...91
  - Sunny Garden Veggie Cream Cheeze...92
  - Sunny Green Chili Cream Cheeze...93
  - Sunny Flox (faux lox) Cream Cheeze...94
  - Horseradish Pate...95

- Chips/Breads

  - Sweet Bell Tortilla Chips...97
  - Olive/Onion Tortilla Chips...98
  - Salsa Chips...99

- Pizza Chips...100
- Olive Bread...101
- Pumpernickel Bread...102
- Soft Onion Herb Bread...103
- Soft Honey Wheat Bread...104

- Salads/Salsas

  - Greek Grapes & Cheeze Salad...106
  - Nacho Salad...107
  - Best Burger Salad...108
  - Russian Dressing...109
  - Sunny Sour Cream...109
  - Coleslaw...110
  - Raw Mayo...111
  - Mustard "Potato" Salad...112
  - Green Pea Salad...113
  - Carrot Raisin Slaw...113
  - Mediterranean Salad...114
  - Creamy Spinach Salad...115
  - Habanero Solar Salsa...116
  - Pineapple Mango Salsa...117
  - Pico de Gallo...117
  - Guacamole...118
  - Creamy Tomatillo Salsa...118
  - Tomatillo Salsa...119
  - Tomato Salsa...119
  - Cranberry Relish...120

- Entrees/Wraps

PREFACE

Necessity is the mother of invention – we've all heard it. Some of us are living it. My experience would be the latter. Money was really tight for us when I finally went raw – recently relocated, only one of us working while I finished with my classes, and bills piling up on us. We had to learn to tighten our belts and make it work FOR us, rather than against us! All this and going 100% raw vegan, too! But how? On such a tight budget? We could barely make the bills in time to deter the disconnects or vehicle repossession. There was little or no money left at the end of our bills for food or even basic necessities.

I took action. I refused to be forced back into beans, rice, pasta, white bread, etc. as is the common dietary dilemma for those of us living on or near the poverty level! Cooked foods make me feel heavy, bloated, lethargic and arthritic. I told my husband that I couldn't do the cooked lifestyle anymore, and that I would gladly water fast to cut costs. I also told him I wanted $10 every 3 days to provide what little food I could find for us to supplement the water fasting. He agreed to my challenge.

Soon I became amazed by just how much I could make that $10 stretch for the two of us! I went into this thinking we'd have nothing but tiny little mono-meals. What I found out, was that if you shop mindfully, really look at what you're buying and establish within your mindset that you're only buying for a few days, you can actually come out pretty well! I began really looking at what I was buying, and thinking about what we still had at home that I could pair with it to make actual FOOD! Frame this as the Raw Iron Chef experience of Frugal Raw Living!

As I was working on preparing our raw foods for the day that morning in late September, I had a thought strike me...I'm doing very well so far for us on this $10:3 day raw food budget. But I think a big part of this is that I am very gifted with knowing what to do with food to make an impressive and palatable presentation. My mom always said a true chef can make something incredible out of almost nothing.

That's what I always strive to do. If it looks good, odds are it will taste good, or can be made to.

My thoughts then glided over to how many people (including myself) have shied away from raw living. How many have deferred back to cooked foods out of what is misconceived as necessity - say, for instance, a seemingly impossible financial crisis. I'm here to tell you that you STILL have to eat. Regardless of your financial situation, the key is to make the most of the money that you do have. Maybe there isn't a full-blown financial crisis...perhaps the situation is more simple than that...it just doesn't seem to fit into the budget with what everyone else in the house wants...so what happens...we give in and go back to their cooked, miserable, unhealthy lives.

IT DOESN'T HAVE TO BE THIS WAY!

Low income living DOES NOT have to mean compromising your health and future on preservatives and fillers!

Then I realized that there's not much out there (book-wise) that tells you how to live raw in a frugal way.

I'd wanted to write a un-cookbook, and I needed an angle to approach it from. So, I got to thinking...what if I write a book on just that - "Frugal Raw" and include not just recipes, but tips to help others learn how raw food can be stretched, how to be inventive with only the supplies at hand – and how to live this healthy lifestyle without finding yourself in the poor house!

I am not a nutritionist, a doctor, or in the health profession. I am a certified Raw Chef, an Artist and an Author who has lived the research for this book, created these cost-effective mouth-watering raw and living recipes, and I present my knowledge, experience and opinions now to you...

The ritual of sharing a meal is a very integral part of familial day-to-day lives, and by nature, people are often challenged and frightened by things outside of their personal "norm."   Have you ever noticed how people react when a vegetarian (of any kind) makes their lifestyle choice known, and then watched or experienced the plethora of negative reactions that ensue? How many people have immediately said in response that they "could never do x-y-or z" and then go into a laundry list of "why nots" of excuses for themselves, when YOU didn't ASK...all you were trying to do was share with them how your lifestyle choices are doing you well? Ever wonder why that is?

It's because people tend to personalize what's happening around them, and they don't want to be put in a situation that they believe would make them uncomfortable or one in which they would feel deprived by – and in this case, it is frugal raw veganism that causes such concern. Removing fluffy white bread, meat, dairy products, refined sugars, etc from your lifestyle can be a challenge not only to you, but those around you as well, if for no other reason.

This is where your personal decision making process should begin and end. You've done the research: you've made your decision, and you are beginning your transition to a beautiful, physically and spiritually enlightening healing lifestyle of raw vegan living. If you are a single person, living alone, you have only yourself to answer to regarding these choices. But what if there are others in your household who don't hold to your new found vision?   A significant other? What about children? How about teenagers?

The best frugal answer I have found when living in a split household, is to make what you are eating as part of the meal that everyone shares. Not only is this economical, and therefore the frugal way of approaching things, this provides the sense of closeness and community we seek when we partake of sharing a meal with our loved ones. Never be judgmental about what others are or are not eating. Do not "stiffen" because others aren't jumping on the raw vegan bandwagon just because you say it's a good thing to do. Have patience and be non-confrontational about it. They will see the positive changes in you – the glow, the peace, and someday, if they're ready, they'll come to it too.

When I first became a vegetarian, I was living with my husband and my eldest son who was then in his early twenties. They were both omnivorous, so meals were at times very frustrating, as I would make "their" food, and "my" food. My husband would say, sorry honey – I don't think I could ever give up meat – later he would say that about dairy, and then about bread as shortly thereafter he would let them go by his own choosing in his own time.   Cooking two separate meals for each meal was taxing and costly! That's when I realized that I could cook my vegetarian meals for all of us, and fix their meat for them as a side dish. It was a much changed mindset from the SAD way of life which focuses on meat as the main part of the meal. This made my cooking life easier, but it was still sometimes restrictive, as my son is a very picky eater. He is neither a lover of vegetables nor fruits.

So, I compromised…I would prepare a starchy vegetable or bread that I knew my son would eat and a couple of veggies I wanted, as well as their meat sides. This finally worked. I would make meals that I would enjoy, where only one or two of the components would require an alternative: tacos, are a great example, and would apply as a meal that can be served as both cooked omni and raw vegan. As a cooked vegan, I would prepare a pan of black beans to replace the meat for myself, and also use a can of black beans in with my co-residents' taco meat to stretch their meal. But to better illustrate how to do this from a raw vegan perspective, consider that all of the basic garnishing components are raw – avocado, onion, tomato, peppers, lettuce, and pico de gallo...and if you want to get fancy, you can prepare a nut-based sour cream. In our split household, I would have what I wanted as a standard preparation of the meal. I could grind up and season some nuts or seeds for my "meat" to roll up in the lettuce leaves with the other garnishes, and would only need to add a small pan of taco meat and corn or flour tortillas for the omnis to be happy too. We would sit together and share the meal without me having to eat everything they were eating. Sometimes, my kids would even want to try what I was eating. This made for much less stress in our family meal time. No one felt odd or challenged about me eating differently, because I was still eating components of what they too were eating.

My husband has since become vegan, and is working his way toward 100% raw vegan. It is all a process. None of my now grown children are vegetarian, although my youngest son is almost there. I'm here to counsel them, but not to push. I give them the respect to make their own choices in their own time for how they feel their bodies best perform.

In regards to young children, everyone's needs and situations are different. If your co-parent doesn't agree with you to go raw and therefore have your children go raw, the best that you can hope for is a 50/50 compromise for the child's diet unless the child makes his/her wishes known to eat only the raw foods. Let them try anything they want to try of your raw food diet. Encourage them to eat raw, but if you are living in a split household, keep the peace by showing respect to your co-habitants. Don't slam other's lifestyles to sway your child to your whims. They may never go raw. They may eventually go raw, but that is up to them and for them to do at their pace – not yours.

Teenagers can be picky eaters. They are looking to define themselves, rebelling, and may not be open to your strange new way of living (on the other hand, they may do it for a while just to be reactionary with their peers). Suddenly Mom or Dad or both have stopped cooking their food – you have to admit it would seem strange to a kid who grew up on SAD. Have patience with them, and don't force your choices on them. You can easily prepare your food as a raw dish and then cook some of the same foods for them. This keeps the spending way down. For instance, an Asian-inspired plate of raw vegan wonderment prepared for you: nori rolls and an un-stir-fry can easily find accompaniment with cooked sushi rice nori rolls for others and use portions of the same raw veggies you make your meal with to feed your family by flash cooking theirs in a wok along with some sauce components for the rest of your family's meal. In this scenario, you have only added the sushi rice outside of your raw realm!

Going raw vegan doesn't have to mean creating an artillery bunker at your dining table or living in a food war zone. It isn't impossible to incorporate your choices into the overall presentation. It just takes a little forethought and planning, and you will find that keeping the peace isn't so insurmountable as you had thought.

I made a really big mistake when I first tried to go raw. I thought that raw vegan was synonymous with raw gourmet. I thought that the correct way to live this raw lifestyle was to prepare tedious, expensive dishes, incorporating "super foods" for 3 squares a day every day! Thankfully, that is not the case. My typical day begins with plain, clear, water. Later in the morning I'll have some fruit – perhaps a few bananas in a carob/honey sauce I enjoy. Then later in the afternoon, I'll have a heavier meal, and this could be things such as raw tacos or something more complex I've prepared in my dehydrator.

To the ignorant mind, the words raw vegan usher forth images of carrot sticks, celery ribs, and salads, salads, salads for life. I am here to attest that raw veganism is not about big plates of boring bunny food. It is a lifestyle that will enrich your life physically, emotionally, mentally, and spiritually. It is about converting what you know as cooked cuisine into a raw, rich, nutrient dense super fuel that nourishes you on every level.

When it comes down to it, it is ALL about YOU, and YOU owning that YOU are worthy of the BEST food in the world! The BEST food that is within your budget and means. That's the bottom line to frugal raw living. While I can promise you a world of betterment filled with an explosion of tastes, experiences, and textures without breaking the bank, and that you will feel better, younger, and happier than you ever have in your life, it comes down to your willingness and personal convictions to successfully embrace and benefit from the total experience.

It is up to you to decide to what level you want to take the raw and living foods lifestyle. A person is considered a raw foodist by definition if they make 75% or more of their food consumption raw and living foods. Optimally, 100% is the best and most healthful option, but it is not always attainable for some with health restrictions such as digestive issues that will require a slower integration. That said, something I see all too often in the Raw world, is people beating themselves up over their decisions to dip back into cooked foods. The reality is that this is a journey – and that there will inevitably be bumps in the road.

How much are you willing to do for yourself in your journey to optimum health? Strive for 100% if that is what you want, but do not feel like you have to hit the reset button on having gone raw each time you make the conscientious choice to partake of a cooked food item or meal. Eventually, if you go 100% raw, you will no longer want cooked foods. For me it took about 6 months, but everyone differs in this.

Living the frugal raw foods lifestyle sometimes means making allowances – but doesn't any lifestyle change? What sort of allowances, you ask? Not buying all organics for one. While organics are optimal, you are still doing yourself betterment just by living this lifestyle the best way that you are financially able. I do not buy all organics, and frankly, some items are not available in organic. Periodically, lists are published of the top 10 or 12 most contaminated food items on the market, and these are the items I consider worthy of note. It is these things you should focus on to buy in organic whenever you can. In a list dated February 2008, the current list encompasses: beef, milk, coffee, peaches, apples, bell peppers, celery, strawberries, lettuces, imported grapes, potatoes, and tomatoes. Only 8 or 9 of those really apply to the raw vegan lifestyle if living it 100%.

Bear in mind too, that a good vegetable wash will clean away many of the impurities and toxins found on standardly grown fruits and vegetables. I also buy from local farmers whenever the opportunity is made available. I do these things and I do not stress over it because I know I am doing so much better for myself than I otherwise would on even a cooked vegan (or otherwise) lifestyle.

Another allowance is that I rarely ever buy anything prepackaged. I try to always make everything myself, rather than buying expensive powders, snack bars, breads, crackers, etc. I buy my nuts, seeds, and flax from a bulk foods store by the pound. This way, I only buy what I will need for a given period. You will notice also that many of my recipes call for either sunflower seeds ($1.39/lb) or cashews ($5.79/lb), and on occasion pecan meal ($2.99/lb) in lieu of the more expensive nuts found in so many gourmet raw recipes. I have found that these two nuts and the pecan meal in particular, I can buy the least expensively, and knowing how to use them effectively expands my uncooking repertoire. Cashews I sometimes buy at local Indian markets. Raw, ground cashews are often used as a thickener in Indian cuisine – especially in cream sauces. I opt for the bags of pieces, rather than whole, as this too is a cost saver. Stores such as this are also where I buy most of my spices.

I will more often than not opt for whole spice and grind it myself in a coffee grinder. This process serves to give your dishes the best flavoring for use of the least amount of spice. Dried herbs and ground spices have shorter shelf lives when it comes to their flavor and potencies. Grinding them fresh releases their oils and aromatic essences. When using a dried herb, always crush and rub it between your hands to awaken the flavors, and you will find that you need less.

Let's talk about raw olives. Some I have seen online priced relatively fairly at just under $7 - $10 for 11 ounces – packed in oil, the jar will weigh a full pound. I like to buy locally whenever I can, so

I have educated myself on what types are raw due to their curing process, and where I can get them. Mediterranean shops will often have the oil-cured variety in stock. You can recognize these by their appearance. They are deep black, wrinkled, appear crushed, and are preserved in olive oil. The curing process begins with fresh, raw, usually pitted black olives that are packed in salt until they begin to break down. Then they are removed from the salt and packaged in olive oil. I have been lucky enough recently to find them in my grocer's deli area. These are priced at $7.99 per pound, and I will usually buy ¼ to ½ a pound at a time which is comprised of mostly olives and I am paying for very little oil with no shipping fees.

As for the "super foods" I rarely, if ever, buy them. I instead focus my buying ability on fresh, whole, raw foods. While I will not pretend to dispute the validity of the nutrients carried in "super foods," I for one, cannot afford them, and frankly refuse to pay for what smacks of a heavily price-driven marketing campaign on only recently made available, and in some cases not fully tested, imported foods.

The founders of the Raw movement didn't have access to these "super foods," and many of them have been living a raw and living foods lifestyle for better than 20 years. Some of them advocate against the use of some of the "super foods" that have been on the market for only a short period of time. While it is true that probably for each raw guru who is opposed to these "super foods," there are an equal number who are in favor and push the sales of them, I am of the opinion that the jury is still out, and that acceptance of their use is best left on a case-by-case basis.

I have read that Jeremy Saffaron, who has been in the Raw Food movement for over 30 years, was the first person to introduce raw cacao to the U.S. market back in 2001. He then pulled it from his shelves after a year and a half of study on its toxicity, and now recommends using it only for medicinal, sacred, or entertainment usage only – not as any kind of daily consumed health food. My advice to incorporating these foods into your diet is to research them fully – good and bad reports before you decide whether to lay your money down for them. Ultimately, it is a matter of personal choice and financial ability.

In regards to things that I would rarely ever use, such as cacao, I don't mind on the odd rare occasion, the use of unsweetened cocoa powder instead (at less than $8 a pound and used in many a raw vegan recipe before raw cacao powder hit the market 7 years ago which currently sits at $22/lb) and for a very brief time dipping down to 99.9% raw. I'm not sold on cacao being as healthy a choice as it is purported to be by its marketers, especially not at its current costliness. Because of this, I consider the use of unsweetened cocoa powder one of the allowances I make on special occasions.

I have also found that I like carob (as its own thing – not as a chocolate replacement but as an alternative) after having believed I did not, and at 1/3 more protein, less fat, no caffeine, and at only 26% ($5.79/lb) of the price of raw cacao powder, I recommend trying it.

When it comes to a choice between raw honey and raw agave, I have found raw local honey to be my best buy – research these items in your own area and see where your best pricing falls before making a buying decision. Honey is found at its best price when bought directly from a local bee keeper rather than a store. Look for terms such as: cold filtered, unprocessed, unpasteurized, and/or unrefined on the labels. I can buy a 44 ounce jar of raw local honey for only $6.98 or about 16 cents per ounce. Whereas the best price in my area on raw agave is $7.49 for only 24 ounces, or 31 cents per ounce. Honey is significantly thicker than agave nectar, and for consistency in recipes that call for agave, I thin the honey by measuring out 1/3 c. honey and adding water to the ½ cup level for every ½ cup needed.

I don't use goji berries. I tried them once and really didn't care for them. At $25 a pound, they'd better be really impressive for me to lay out that kind of money! I much prefer getting my antioxidants from the plethora of other dark blue and red fruits and vegetables readily and locally available for a fraction of the cost, by which I instead enjoy fresh blueberries, beets, raspberries, blackberries, dark grapes, and pomegranates to name only a few.

There are other amazingly expensive powders in the super foods realm, such as Maca at $32.00 for a kilo (2.2 lbs)...a purported sexual enhancer and fertility herb. Fo-Ti or Ho Shou Wu, another vitality herb, runs $45.86 per pound. I find I live my frugal raw vegan life well without these things. My advice to those needing to live frugally but wanting to try these costly items would be to build the cost into your budget on a week when you might have a surplus of regular foods and can afford the hit. Due to their expense, I don't recommend trying to incorporate these as staple items in your home.

Successfully living the frugal raw lifestyle also means learning staggered meal planning, which allows for a "roll" on recommended raw staples and using everything you have before you buy more. Learn to reuse what you create as components to create new dishes or experiences. For instance, a batch of dehydrator-style raw vegan burgers can be used for: burgers or specialty sandwiches, to fill enchiladas, top salads, be broken apart and used to create a "meat" sauce for raw pastas, stroganoffs, and gravies! A batch of raw "refried beans" made in your food processor can be used for carrot or corn chip nachos, to stuff peppers, for tacos, burritos, and also to top various

Tex-Mex themed salsa'd salads. To be frugally raw-minded is to think outside of the box so that nothing goes to waste, which will keep your platters varied and interesting without exacting unwonted expense.

Knowing how to make last-minute substitutions with the ingredients you have on-hand is imperative. To gain this knowledge, it is vital to know what items will do in their original form versus what you can effectively make them do for you. An example of this would be in making a tomato-based marinade sauce, and finding yourself without dried tomatoes, which standardly serve as a thickener. Knowing what other dried fruits can also be used for the same purpose will serve you well in this manner. See Chapter 7 for guidelines on ingredient functionality.

Lastly, something I do for myself periodically as a practice, is I will water-only fast for about a day or day and a half. Anyone interested in starting this practice should ease into it to determine when they should break the fast. This is a good, holistic practice to get into, as it allows your body's digestive system to rest and to keep itself in optimal condition. It also serves to help flush out lingering toxins. Ayurvedic medicine prescribes this practice be done once a week, every week, and on the same day each week. I tend to do it once or twice a month. The fact that it helps to also save on groceries from time-to-time is an additional boon for the frugal raw foodist.

The Right Tools

The implements that are truly necessary for living the raw food lifestyle are a good knife, a cutting board, a coffee grinder, a food processor, and a blender. Those are the tools with which I began my raw journey. Recently, a dehydrator has been added, which while it does increase the variety in your food scope, it is not a necessity for going raw. I also recently came to own a spiral slicer. All have been acquired in good and due time. Fine mesh sieve-type colanders are also excellent investments if you wish to get into sprouting grains and seeds. The purchase of any tool should be weighed for the investment.

The good news is that there are a number of raw food cookbooks that purposefully do not call for the use of a dehydrator because not everyone can afford the investment. Furthermore, your body will love you more, the more juicy, fresh, living foods and pure clean water you give it. Dehydrator usage should be kept to a minimum, so as not to encourage water-weight gain and fluid retention. Also, dehydrated fruits have a very high sugar concentration that can be promote tooth decay.

The Right Tool: What you will be preparing will dictate the necessity for certain tools...

I.   Quality Knife – is an absolute must have, and quite often can be the only tools you use. Make sure that your knife is well-balanced, has a dependable blade, and is safely set in the handle. Avoid knives whose blades bend or wiggle or those that have fragile plastic handles. The choice of knife is a very personal thing and each person will have their own preferences. Our household knives are made by J. A.

Henkels, and some are priced over $100. Ours were gifts. I have found the Anolon Brunello collection knives to be an excellent buy and in an excellent price range – some being only $25. These knives are excellently balanced, have wooden handles and thick blades that hold their edges well. An excellent choice for the Frugal Raw Vegan!

II.   Cutting Boards – While I prefer a good, solid, wooden board, preferably of bamboo, hygienically speaking, the non-wood boards are not known to trap bacteria as they are usually without pores. If you are living in a house divided, and have omnis in the house, you will be better served by a non-wooden board. Flexible and synthetic boards are inexpensive – usually less than $10 for a set; the flexible ones being sold in multi-colored sets of five. Another alternative is marble which, while beautiful, they can be very cumbersome and heavy and you should be prepared for the occasional high-pitched squeak when slicing away!

III. Coffee Grinder – use to grind whole spices and nuts to a powder. I own a kitchenaid grinder, which has a metal cylinder which protects the unit when I am grinding hard spices such as cinnamon sticks. These usually cost around $25. This will pay for itself as you learn to buy whole spices in bulk to grind to powders.

IV.   Food Processor – These range from $20 to over $200. Mine is mid-range – a 7-cup kitchenaid that cost about $90, which we bought a couple of years ago. The thing to bear in mind with the purchase of a food processor, is what your intentions are for it. If you plan on processing dates, sundried tomatoes, and unsoaked nuts, you will want to purchase one with a higher horsepower than the $20 models. I have found that the $20 models tend to burn out very easily if used for anything more than a quick chopping of vegetables or fresh fruits.   If homemade nut butters are your desire, go for a higher end model, or a high-powered blender. Also, size is an important issue. I have found at times, that my 7-cup pitcher is too small for some of the standardly offered recipes, and I wind up transferring it by component to a mixing bowl for final fusion. In food processors, you would want to make tings such as pates, salsas, guacamole, burgers, bread, and cookie doughs.

V.   Blender – A high-powered, high dollar blender ($350 and up) is not necessary, but is a nice thing to have for making soups, sauces, smoothies, and desserts smooth and creamy. If you use a standard blender, be wary of putting anything very hard or tough into it, and soak all nuts overnight before attempting to process them in your blender. Also, refrain from putting stemmed items in that could find themselves wrapped around the blade. If making green smoothies, stick to fruits and soft leaves – no ribs, seeds or citrus rind unless you are using a high-powered blender such as a VitaMix or K-Tec. We bought our VitaMix on a 3-month installment plan about 3 years ago, and have loved and appreciated it ever since.

VI.   Dehydrators: The crème de la crème of food dehydrators has an adjustable temperature switch, allowing you to keep the drying temp at or below 108 degrees, and has the heat element and the fan in the back of the unit. I own the 9-tray Excalibur, and highly recommend it for those who can afford the investment. The Excalibur comes in three sizes: 4, 5, and

9 tray. The 4-tray at the time of this writing, usually costs just over $100 but is significantly smaller than the 5 and 9-tray models. The 9-tray is usually about $220. The paraflexx sheets are additional and sold per sheet for approximately $8 each, but I have seen deals online where the sheets are thrown in for free. These will be necessary for when you are dehydrating something very wet that would otherwise drip through the mesh screens. The number of paraflexx sheets to purchase is a decision of personal preference. Dehydrators can be used to make raw pizzas, breads, chips, cookies, crackers, burgers, and also to warm or remove the chill from refrigerated items. Also, if you live in a dry, sunny climate, you can make sun-drying boxes to use outside instead.

VII. Spiral Slicers: These are often also called Spiroolis or Saladaccos, and they safely replace the want of a mandolin slicer. They range from $25 to $30 and are good for making paper thin slices of root vegetables for raw raviolis, and potato, yam, and zucchini chips if you have a dehydrator. This device also produces angel hair pastas from zucchini, summer squash, etc.

VIII. Fine Mesh Colanders: These can be had for as little as $7 each in some retail stores. Look for them too in Indian markets! I recently bought one for only $9 that has four interchangeable mesh screens, each having a different gauge size to the mesh. This allows you to choose the best size mesh for the size seed(s) that you are sprouting. They allow you to rinse and drain the sprouts in the same container they mature in, and help to keep them from molding due to the availability of air flow. Sprouted grains and seeds can be used in salads, to make hummus, to create a side dish, or make dehydrator breads, cookies, and crackers.

IX.   Hand Tools: There are an amazing amount of gadgets on the market these days that make our raw lives much easier for very little money. Some of these include:

- Citrus reamers: this is a singly hand-held device that has a juicing point end. It is an excellent tool for those who do not have a citrus juicer. These cost about $4 each.

- Vegetable peelers: a must have in ANY kitchen, and odds are that you already own one. Can be used for not only peeling, but also for thin slicing squash and root veggies for raw pasta, lasagna, raviolis, and chip preparation if you don't own/want to buy a spiral slicer. Cost usually ranges from $1 to $8.

- Julienne peelers: Excellent for making spaghetti from soft squash, and matchsticks from apples and root vegetables like carrots and beets. Standard cost is about $7.

- Melon ballers: I use mine not just for melon, but also for hollowing out apple halves and tomatoes when I want to stuff them. Standard cost is $2-$3.

- Ripple slicers: I don't know how else to describe this, but it is a small manual blade with a handle for the top side. The blade itself is wavy. I use it for slicing root veggies for nachos, BBQ, and dipping "chips." I bought mine at Linens N Things, and it cost about $3.

- Basting brush: Good to have if you are making veggie skewers, marinated, or BBQ veggies in your dehydrator.

You will want to continue to add flavor as the veggies soften. These can sometimes be found in dollar stores!

- Lettuce knife: A wonderful plastic knife that can be used to cut lettuces or to chiffonade spinach or herbs and the greens won't turn brown! Metal knives turn lettuce edges an unappetizing brown color. Can be purchased for around $2.00 in some grocery and standard department stores.
- Graters/Microplanes: These will be useful in grating ginger, nutmegs, zesting citrus fruits, and root vegetables.

X.   Mixing Bowls: I prefer stainless steel, glass, or pyrex as plastic (unless melanine) tends to take on flavors and stain due to its porous nature. Stores such as Linens N Things carry sets of 3 or 4 stainless steel mixing bowls for sometimes less than $15. Warehouse stores such as Sam's Club will also sometimes have deals on sets of these. In addition, I have found these types of bowls in discount closeout-type stores on occasion.

XI.   Colander: These come in a wide array of sizes, styles, and materials. They can be bought in dollar stores as well as high-end shops and most places in-between. It isn't necessary to spend top dollar on them so long as you get a size that works for you. I currently have 3, all of which are enameled metal. I find I often use more than one in my raw food preparations.

XII.   Lettuce spinner: These do not have to be expensive. I have seen them priced from about $3 up to $40! Mine is one of the $3 variety that I purchased at Walmart. It isn't fancy, but it WORKS. I like these devices, as it is the degree of wetness that will dictate the shelf life of your greens. Excess moisture causes lettuces to wilt or go bad before you have a chance to use them. This device will pay for itself almost immediately, when buying and successfully storing lettuces by the head - a definite cost saver when a 1 pound head of leaf or romaine lettuce will average $1.99 or less, while a half pound bag of prepared salad lettuce will run at times more than $3.00.

Storing Raw and Living Foods

      Proper treatment and storage of raw and living foods is critical in keeping your lifestyle successfully frugal. I have often heard people, especially singles, say that their produce goes bad on them before they use it all. There are two basic principles to bear in mind with regard to the raw and living foods lifestyle:

      1.   When purchasing time-sensitive raw fruits and vegetables such as some greens, tomatoes, bananas, peaches, etc. buy only what you will use within 3 or 4 days.

      2.   Store each item properly.

Below are my recommendations for maximizing the shelf life of your raw and living foods:

1. Bananas: Store at room temperature **only** if planning on eating fresh. Refrigeration will turn the peels black. Don't bother with the banana stands – I once had an entire bunch that committed mass suicide on one and had to use the lot of them in smoothies! Instead, store on a dry shelf or in a colander to allow for air flow. Prime time for eating bananas is when they just begin to freckle. If freezing for ice creams or smoothies, peel and cut them up beforehand and store in a freezer-safe container to avoid freezer burn.

2. Peaches, Plums, Nectarines, and other pitted thin-skinned fruits: Store at room temperature, and rotate daily if kept in a bowl, basket, or colander. These can also be prepped (stones removed and cut up) and frozen if placed in proper containers.

These fruits will ripen quickly and consequently have a higher spoilage rate, hence the need for rotation.

3. Grapes: Always in the refrigerator, and preferably in a crisper drawer. They will dry out easily and begin to shrivel if left sitting in the open air.

4. Lemons/Limes: Store in the refrigerator. They will keep longer and won't dry out as fast. Before cutting, press and roll the fruit on a hard surface to break up the juice cells. If zesting, do so prior to cutting and juicing.

5. Oranges/Grapefruits/Tangerines: Store at room temperature and keep well ventilated to allow them to continue to ripen.

6. Melons: Are fine at room temperature until serving. Watch for any development of weak spots in the rind. Once cut open, they must be refrigerated.

7. Tomatoes: NEVER refrigerate tomatoes if you can avoid it. Tomatoes lose flavor and become mealy and unappetizing when refrigerated. Instead, store them in a cool, dry place at room temperature and cut up or prepare only what you will realistically use that day. Buy ripe tomatoes in small quantities, and a few less ripe for later in the week.

8. Lettuces: Buy by the head, not the bag – and wash it as soon as you get it home. Leave it in whole leaves or tear it into salad and spin it predominantly dry before putting it away. Lettuces that

have been broken up for salads can be stored in Ziploc-style baggies in the refrigerator – air tightness is key. Leaves are best stored in oblong sealable plastic containers wrapped in a clean kitchen towel to reduce moisture.

9. Greens (collards, kale, spinach): Store in airtight containers or leave produce bagged and in crisper drawers to avoid wilting/drying leaves. I use collards most often for veggie wraps, so as soon as I bring them home, I like to wash each leaf and store them with paper toweling between the layers of leaves in a large plastic container in the fridge. This really speeds up making meals of tacos, veggie wraps, dolmas, and the like when you don't have to wait for your wraps to dry!

10. Mushrooms: Best stored in the refrigerator in brown paper sacks. If bought in a cello pak, remove them from it and pace into a paper sack. Too much air will cause them to wrinkle and dry, and too much moisture will cause them to sour and mold. The paper sack will equalize their environment for a maximum shelf life.

11. Onions/Garlic/Potatoes/Yams: Are best stored dry. I keep mine in wicker baskets on shelves in my kitchen. Leftover onions are put in Ziploc-style bags or air-tight containers and refrigerated. Do not place onions on the top shelf of the refrigerator, as the high water-content of onions will cause them to freeze.

12.   Peppers: Keep them in plastic bags and store in crisper drawers. These also have a high moisture content, so store cut peppers in the same fashion as onions/garlic.

13.   Ginger root, Carrots, Parsnips: Refrigerate to keep them from getting limp and dried out. I prefer to keep my ginger root in the closed butter keeper shelf in my fridge door. Carrots and parsnips I place in the crisper drawers.

14.   Avocados: Store at room temperature. Avocados ripen best when not in the refrigerator. If you happen to cut an avocado open before "its time," close it back up and place it in a brown paper sack for a couple of days. If you only use a half, "paint" the exposed flesh with raw mayo and store in an airtight container to retard discoloration. When selecting avocados, grasp the fruit firmly and press on the stem end with your thumb. A ripe one will be firmly soft – not mushy. If the sides give easily, it is too ripe.

15.   Salads: Are best stored separately as components in air-tight containers. If making a tossed-type of salad, only take from the containers what you are going to realistically use for that meal. You can always toss up a little more in seconds if you need to. For non-tossed salads, build them directly onto each serving plate from the separate components.

16.   Sprouts: After successfully sprouting seeds, grains, or beans, dry them and place in air-tight containers (I use zip-loc type bags) in the refrigerator if you are not going to use them

immediately. They will (in some cases) continue to mature but at a slower rate. Always smell them before use. If they have a sourness or acridity to them, **do not use**, as they have gone rancid due to improper rinsing/drainage during the sprouting phase, or they have been merely kept too long.

17.   Nuts: Dry nuts can be stored at room temperature or refrigerated. I prefer to keep mine in an old bread box. Soaked nuts can be drained and stored in airtight containers in the refrigerator for a few days prior to use.

18.   Young Coconuts: ALWAYS store in the refrigerator. Leaving them out will accelerate spoilage. When purchasing, take care to look for spots of mold on the outer husk. If molding, do not buy. Young coconut flesh will vary in color from a translucent jelly-like pinkish-beige to purple, to full-on white as it begins to mature and the flesh thickens. If grey and malodorous, do not use, as it has gone rancid.

19.   Mangoes: Store well in or out of the refrigerator. I have bought these cheaply by the case, and have successfully stored some for up to a month in my refrigerator. Look for fruits that have deep color, firm, smooth skin, and only a faint softness.

Staples of a Frugal Raw Vegan Kitchen

There are certain raw foods that we consider staples in our house. This will also vary based on what your level of raw food living you intend to practice. I like to keep the following items on hand, which are standardly used in non-dehydrator recipes:

Raw Sunflower Seeds

Raw Cashews

Raw Pumpkin Seeds

Raw Sesame Seeds

Raw Honey

Medjool Dates

Organic Raisins

Bananas

Onions

Lemons or Limes (whichever is the better deal, usually)

Garlic

Miso

Nutritional Yeast

Nut meals (pre-ground nuts from bulk bin areas – these can be used for pates, pie crusts, etc – and are significantly less expensive than buying the whole nut)

Ground, cold-milled flax seeds

Raw Apple Cider Vinegar

Cold-pressed Olive Oil

Raw Tahini

Bragg's Liquid Aminos

Things to add to this list if you are going to go the dehydrator route would be:

Whole Flax Seeds

Soft Wheat Berries

Buckwheat Groats

Rye Berries

Economical Modifications and Uncooking On the Fly!

Knowing your ingredients' functionality will carry you a long way in being able to work with what you have and what you can afford.

Sunflower Seeds: Coarsely chop dry for a "meatier" texture to use as taco "meat" and the like. Soak overnight for use in creamy creations such as pates, cheezes, sauces, and sour creams. Sunflower seeds make an excellent substitute for almonds at as much as an 85% cost per pound savings.

Cashews: A very creamy seed, especially if soaked overnight. Very mild flavor – lends itself well to dishes of a sweeter variety – desserts especially, and exotic creamy sauces/gravies as are found in Indian cuisine.   These are great to use in place of the more costly macadamias and Brazil nuts due to their creamy texture and unimposing flavor.

Nut Meals: I have found nut meals in various bulk bin areas. These are perfect for dishes in which nuts/seeds are to be ground to a powder such as pates, crusts, brownies, breads, crackers, etc. Pecan meal especially, substitutes well for costly walnuts – whole or pieces!

Young Coconuts: The flesh of one plus 1/3 c. of the coconut water makes an excellent custard base when paired with a few bananas. This will produce a very firm custard that is sliceable! Use the entire coconut (water and flesh) as a soup base for creamy soups such as mushroom, carrot ginger, and tomato. Also can be used in smoothies.

Bananas: Can be used to thicken or bind smoothies, puddings, and custards. If frozen, they are also a great ice cream base. Bananas are the most cost-efficient fruit in cost per pound.

Miso – used in making nut cheezes – the one ingredient that makes the difference between making a cheeze and preparing a pate. Not a live food, but beneficial due to the fermentation enzymes it carries. I buy "mild" or "white" in small quantities.

Dried tomatoes – use to enhance tomato flavor and to thicken sauces, soups, and condiments. Check for use of sulfer products, and choose non-sulfered or dry your own in a dehydrator or sun-drying box. Best tomato for this is the Roma, which is most cost effectively purchased in the summertime. Growing and drying your own is a great option even if only potted and on a patio, as Roma variety tomato plants do not get very large.

Dates – use to sweeten and thicken sauces, creams, and as a base in pie crusts, brownies, and desserts. Dates come in many varieties and flavors. Look for pump, juicy, fresh dates when buying and compare cost per variety.

Raisins – a lighter sweetener than dates. Can be used in making lighter pie crusts, and is usually less expensive per pound than are dates.

Dried fruits: many dried fruits can be used as sweeteners and thickeners. Dried pineapple or papaya could be used to thicken a Caribbean BBQ sauce or chutney in lieu of dates. Tamarind can be used in Mexican, Indian, and Thai cuisines. Dried lemon rinds are used in Greek cuisine as a seasoning.

Ground, cold-milled flax seeds - these are good for thickening a pureed fruit to a jelled consistency for a pie or cake topper or raw donut filler. Also used in making crackers, breads, and chips.

Nutritional Yeast – used as a thickener and to give a cheezy flavor to soups, sauces, and well, cheezes! It is a great source for B-12. Buy in small quantities from the bulk bins. You won't need large amounts of it at a time. I usually go for a ¼ pound at a time.

Olive Oil – will give a richness to a dish much like the use of butter in cooked foods. This is also a good emulsifier when blended for extended periods.

Lemon/Lime Juice – provides a soured taste to nut creams for sour cream as well as gives a richness to nut cheezes, makes an excellent vinaigrette or marinade base.

Lemon/Lime Zest - the finely grated colored part of the peel of the lemon or lime is what gives food the true flavor of the fruit. It has a much stronger scent and therefore heightened olfactory impression. Take care to not grate into the white pith, as this will produce a bitterness in the dish. Use anytime you want to make a lemon/lime impact with a dish.

Bragg's Liquid Aminos – use in place of the more expensive and harder to find raw Nama Shoyus. Bragg's has a similar soy sauce taste to it.

Tahini – a good base for creamy salad dressings and mustards, and is also an ingredient used in sour cream to give it more body.

Now that you have an understanding on these basic ingredients and their properties, you should come to discern how to use them to your utmost frugal advantage. For instance, you now know that you can use sunflower seeds in lieu of almonds. This increases your buying power greatly! Also, you have an understanding of what you need to do to manipulate the ingredients to create the desired effect in your cuisine.

When uncooking on the fly, you will often find that the current market will tend to advocate what supplies you have at hand from one shopping trip to the next. This is where your personal creativity comes into play. Consider the flavors of each food within your scope, and decide whether they will compliment each other or if they might clash. Bear in mind also, what spices you have at home to combine with these potential purchases before you buy. Begin your uncooking process in the Produce department before you ever get to the registers. Use your mind's eye and your memory of the taste, smell, and textures of each food when making your buying choices. Doing this will hone your culinary skills and sharpen your abilities to stay frugally raw! Consider your shopping challenges to be your personal Raw Iron Chef competition…

Shopping & Green Living – Tricks and Tips that Save You $$

Some of the recommendations to cut cost on the raw food lifestyle that are flying all over the internet include buy in bulk, by the case, or buy damaged produce from your local grocer. While these are all very good ways to cut cost if you have a family to feed, if you are single or just a couple and are already on a limited budget, you don't have the money to buy cases and cases of food. What's more, if it is just you or you plus one, odds are, you'll lose some of that case you just saved so much on. You won't be able to eat all of it by yourself, unless that's what you live off of for the duration of the food. Even then, some of it will still go bad unless it is something that will be okay for an extended period in the fridge – like mangoes or young coconuts.

As you progress in your raw journey, you will find that you want/need less food, and on a day-to-day basis, you also want simpler, lighter, juicy fare – mono-meals may even become your preference. But when transitioning, we all want foods that make us feel like we're really having a special treat. Believe it or not, you CAN do this on a limited budget!

What I am going to share with you now, is how I have managed to cut food bill expenses for one or two people over the years, and have successfully educated myself to standardly shop:

I. Asian Markets: At one time, I lived in an area that had many, many Oriental and Indian grocery stores. Produce, spices, almonds, cashews, and sesame seeds are cheapest in these stores by far. At one point, I could buy a case of mangoes for less than $4.00 – these I would buy from time to time, as we used them often, and they do store well in the refrigerator. Young coconuts were $1.19 each. Exotic melons could be had for less than a dollar. Shiitake mushrooms, dried mushroom varieties, seaweeds - again, a fraction of the cost of buying in a main stream store. These are definitely worth checking out if you have any available to you. You won't be able to buy organic, so educate yourself on the farming practices of the different countries. These stores will also give you cost-effective exposure to trying new exotic fruits and vegetables you might only have otherwise found in a high-end gourmet or whole foods store. Buy your spices (whole or ground) in large bags here for pennies by comparison to what you would pay in the mainstream grocery stores. I once bought a 5 lb bag of whole cumin for less than what I would have paid for a standard sized bottle of the same in a grocery store!

II. Farmer's Markets and Produce Stands: ALWAYS cheaper than the grocery store, and some venders will be willing to sell a case of a specific food for their own cost or only slightly over. I have to admit, I was spoiled. The market I once knew was open 365 days a year! Furthermore, it was HUGE and only about 20 minutes away from y home. It was housed in three warehouse-sized open barracks. There were local growers, growers from Mexico, Importers, and Interstate distributors. It was where all of the area restaurants would go to stock up on their daily needs. There were other smaller farmer's markets around town, at some of which were certified organic growers. Check your local farmer's markets association for locations and availabilities in your area.

III.   Buying organics in the grocery store. I buy organic whenever feasible, but don't stress too hard over my non-abilities. In those cases, I use a good vegetable wash. I have a simple formula I use to keep my budget in check – if the organics are no more than 10 cents per pound more than the non-organics, I buy the organics. I have found that some of the organics offered in grocery stores are only a few cents more than standardly grown produce.   An example of this is that I always opt for organic carrots at 99 cents per pound over standardly grown carrots at 87 – 95 cents per pound.

IV.   Talk to the Produce Managers of your local stores about letting you buy the produce they do not feel that they can sell. It should be priced at pennies on the dollar, as you will probably have to cut away some gashes and bruises, but you should still be left with good amounts that are usable.

V.   Grow Your OWN! I cannot tell you how easy, fun, rewarding and cost-effective growing your own organic fruits and vegetables is! Easy to grow items are lettuce, tomatoes, peppers, cucumbers (homemade pickle variety is a nice compact plant), basil, oregano, and mint. Our first garden was simple, and of the salad variety. We grew 6 varieties of tomatoes, 5 kinds of peppers, two types of cucumbers, in addition to an herb garden. I had tomatoes and peppers until mid-December when non-growers were paying upwards of $4 per pound for tomatoes! Having this garden was little work, and well worth the effort in savings. If you live in an apartment, you can still grow your own – in deep trench pots you can make yourself. Broken pallets can sometimes be had for free, and you are just a hammer and nails away from a proper gardening plot! Make the growing boxes 1' – 2' deep, 3' long, and 1' – 2' wide. Drill ¼" to ½" holes in the bottom of these boxes and install "feet" on them to allow proper drainage.

VI. Set a food budget for yourself BEFORE you go grocery shopping, and shop for food ONLY in the produce section. What I have found to work very well for us, is to limit our buying to $10-20 every 3 days; going in and buying the maximum amount of what I could find on sale (which is usually those items in peak season), and then just getting creative with whatever I have been able to procure. If you want to make a specific dish, only make 1 - 2 of the more elaborate fare per week. Often these recipes will make enough for multiple meals, and some can be converted to new creations. Keep the rest of your meals simple – smoothies, soups, salads, sunflower seed pates rolled up in collard, lettuce, or cabbage leaves as veggie rolls or raw tacos!

V. Bananas, bananas, bananas! They are easily the least expensive item (per pound) in the entire produce section, and they're not only filling, they are nutritionally packed! Make these a staple item on your grocery list, and look also for the

Manager's Special bags on these from time to time. The last one I bought had 17 bananas in it – for only 99 cents! This bag weighed 6.6 pounds, and I only had to throw 1 of the bananas away due to pre-buy damage. Most had been put in the bag because they were singles that were no longer attached to a bunch.

VI. Frozen Fruits/Veggies – while these are not optimal nutritionally speaking, (fresh is best) but these are great supplementary items outside of the normal growing seasons. They are picked at their peak, and the frozen, and sometimes actually have a higher nutrient density than the fresh out of season fare. I use frozen fruit in smoothies, frozen corn and green peas in salads and entrees, and in some dehydrated items.

VII. ALWAYS look for "Manager's Special" items and 10 for $10 sales. Many times, the manager's specials are done on bagged salads (the ONLY time I will buy them), cello pak mushrooms, and even organics are sometimes put on 10 for $10 sales! Talk to your Produce Manager to see if there is a particular pattern to the markdowns so you don't miss out!

VIII. Nut Substitutions: I see numerous raw recipes calling for high dollar nuts. I have found that many times, they are easily substitutable if you know what to do with the subs and which ones to use. Raw sunflower seeds are the most economical value. These can be used for making anything from burgers, to cheezes, to sauces, to desserts! Soaking them will produce a different texture in the final dish than dry grinding. I also like to use raw cashews from time to time for things such as sour cream, cheezes, and mayo. They are a creamier nut than the sunflower seed – especially after soaking. Pumpkin and Sesame seeds are also great to keep on hand and are also wonderfully affordable – use on salads or to garnish dishes for a special kick! Almonds, walnuts, pecans, hazelnuts, macadamias and brazils are all high dollar items, so I keep their usage minimal. I have found, though that some stores offer nut meal – ground pecans, hazelnuts, and sometimes walnuts are to be found in bulk bin areas or in bulk dry good stores for a fraction of the cost of the whole nuts or even the pieces. Most of the recipes that call for nuts, usually involve grinding them to a powder. Save a step and save yourself some serious money! Pecans are usually sold for about $8 per pound, but I can buy the meal for only $3 per pound!

IX.   If you are going to use any oil on a regular basis, stick with cold-pressed olive oil. Flax and coconuts oils (to name a couple) make good supplements for certain health issues, but for day-to-day usage in food preparation, olive oil is your most economical raw food buy. If you choose to incorporate one of the more expensive oils, build it in on a week that it will fit your buying ability.

X.   Raw Honey – buy locally farmed, cold or non-processed, non-filtered honey from local suppliers. You can sometimes get a cut rate by buying direct that you cannot get from a third party grocery store. Buying local honey also provides better allergen relief for pollen sufferers.

XI.   Exercise caution in the buying and use of expensive "super foods." I consider these "fun-time" purchases, and rarely ever buy them. If you feel that you just *have* to have one – make sure you purchase it in one of your buying weeks where you might have more wiggle-room than another, and use it sparingly. These items include: cacao, cacao butter, goji berries, maca, fo-ti, coconut oil, coconut and cacao butter.

XII.   Do not fortify your diet with an abundance of commercially dehydrated fruits. These are usually treated with sulfer dioxide and are much more costly than making your own. Dehydrated fruits are high in concentrated sugars and are bad for your teeth. Dehydrated foods deplete your body of water as they rehydrate through the digestive process. Bear this in mind as you consume these items and up your water intake from what you know to be your minimum.

XIII.   Buy by the case only if you can afford to, and have ways and mean to store and use all of the items. For some of us (1-2 in a household), this just does not always work as well as it does for families. Use your judgment, and buy only what you know you will use within a few days, and at the best price.

XIV. Join a farming co-op! Sweat equity and a small investment will go a long way if you cannot grow your own on your own, then everyone splits the bounty as it is harvested.

XV.   If juicing or making your own nut milks, reserve the pulps for use in making other foods. Carrot pulp can be used to make raw carrot cake. Nut pulps can be used for pates, burgers, and as cookie, cracker, chip, and bread bases. If you don't wish to use it right away, put it in an airtight container in the refrigerator or freezer until you have accumulated enough to utilize.

XVI.   Compost, compost, compost! Never let anything go to waste. Even if you only make a small bin, you'll have a rich soil enhancer you can use in growing foodstuffs in pots or in the ground.

XVII.   Frugal Raw living is green living – buying locally to cut fuel use, using minimal energy to prepare foods, reusing foods to create new dishes and composting what you won't use. It all adds up to a lesser carbon imprint and impact on our world.

Frugal Fitness

Part and parcel in living frugally raw is becoming frugally fit! Not everyone can afford a gym. Fewer still can afford such things as rebounders, bow-flexes, and other such costly toys. Things such as weight benches, treadmills, and stationary bikes are not only costly, but cumbersome and they take up a fair amount of room. I am not saying that any of these things are bad. If a person can afford them, financially and otherwise, they are excellent tools. But what about those of us who don't have these options? What are some cost-efficient ways to do OUR bodies right?

The first thing that comes to mind, and that which has worked excellently for me, is walking. Most people own a comfortable pair of shoes. Measure out a distance on a map or by your car's odometer, and you don't have the need for the expense of a pedometer. Work yourself up to at least 3 miles a day of brisk walking to effectively raise your metabolism. Have a small child at home? Take them with you in their stroller!

For days that I cannot get outside, I have a single dvd for power walking indoors. It came with a resistance belt, and cost only $12.99. In years past, I would stop at a local mall on my way home from work and do laps around he levels and up and down the stairs.

For a lesser price on fitness media, check out your local used book store(s) for fitness tapes/dvds. Look for numerous interests such as Tai Chi, tae bo, belly dance, aerobics, body focus, yoga, etc.

Take up running – do so as a series of alternating walking/slow running distances and build your way up.

Buy a single or set of dumbbells – start with what you feel comfortable using. I chose 5-lbs. I use these each day for my upper body work, but they can also intensify lunges and power walks. Each dumbbell I bought cost only $6. There are a wide variety of types and styles, and therefore prices. Shop around and get the best deal.

Calisthenics. We all did them in gym class – push ups, sit ups, crunches, leg lifts, pull-ups, squats, etc – build them into your daily routine over time. For a fun afternoon, do them in your local park!

Gardening/Yard work: This counts – believe me! In my organic gardening pursuits, I am often clearing land manually with a pick axe, rakes, shovels, etc. Planting is another wonderful sweat producer! After the garden is in, weeding can take a number of hours each week depending on the size of your garden. Develop the opportunities of resistance posing when doing these tasks to stretch and tone.

Most people in Western civilization do not realize that our bodies are actually made to fast. Fasting allows the digestion to have a break, and the energy normally used by the body to digest foods (which, sadly makes up a larger portion of our daily expenditures the worse we treat ourselves: SAD, Cooked, etc.) turns its focus to repairing the body on a cellular level – damaged, diseased cells can be reconstructed and healed through this process…fasting can even cure the body of asthma and allergies! In addition, fasting allows one to get better in touch with their spirituality and their inner selves.

I did a fair amount of research before deciding just how I wanted to plan out my own cleansing period. What I decided was a combination for the full experience. I also intend to do this annually leading up to and including the Spring Equinox. Think about it – when are we the most sedentary? During the colder months of the year. cleansing is an excellent way to move those latent toxins out of your body and give you optimal performance for the playing months! I feel this schedule makes it easier on the body than an all out fasting time as it is transitionary:

3 days of water-only fasting
15 days of raw orange juice feasting
4 -15 days of smoothie/green smoothie feasting
Transition back to solid foods

NOTE: The transition back to solid foods is a slow and conscientious journey. This would begin with small portions of soft fruits and vegetables while still including your smoothies until you are back to your standard amount of solids.

Why smoothies in lieu of juices? Juicing strips the fiber right out of the food and drinking juices are like pouring pure (albeit natural) sugar straight into your body. This can be a shock to those who are hypoglycemic. I prepare my orange juice in my vitamix, retaining all of the fiber. Fiber slows down the distribution of the natural sugars.

Now I will explain my reasoning for each of the transitions of the fasting/feasting period. The first three days (water-only fasting) are the time in which the lion's share of the most dramatic physiological changes occur. During this three day period, the body switches from its primary fuel source (glucose converted from the foods we eat) to another (ketosis – or body fat to create glucose) to finally full on ketone production – the use of fatty acids as fuel instead of glucose. This serves to cause your body to burn fats, expel toxins, and to begin to repair diseased and damaged cells.

The second part of this healing journey is the raw orange juice feasting. Organic oranges are preferable if you can get them as they should contain no toxins, and that's part of what we're getting rid of here! The transition from water-only to the integration of orange juice is entered into cautiously as you transition, as you do not want to dump a huge amount of citric acid into a body that has just been through a 3-day pure cleanse, so introduce it slowly. My method is to put two peeled seeded oranges into my vita mix with one part water and blend until I have juice. This should make about 3 cups. While I am drinking it, I am alternating it with a sip of pure, clean water. I also drink water throughout my day, and only have the orange juice if I am truly hungry.

Orange juice feasting offers many of the benefits of water-only fasting. It is very easy to digest, which is still allowing for your body to have that rest from digesting. It is also not as intense as water-only, because your body is now taking in a food energy, which will allow you to function better physically and mentally rather than consign yourself to resting. This is especially beneficial for those who work a 9-5 job. You can begin your water-only on a Friday, and begin your orange juice intake on Monday before you leave for work. You'll be surprised the dramatic change that occurs just on that first glass of golden elixir!

Fruit itself is a cleansing food, so the orange juice serves to continue to give your cells the same deep cleansing and clears out the toxins, allowing the body to continue in its healing journey. Oranges are nutrient dense foods that are rich in fiber, electrolytes, and water - also containing:

- Vitamins: A, B1, B2, B6, C, and E, biotin, niacin, pantothenic acid, and folic acid.
- Minerals: calcium, copper, iron, magnesium, manganese, phosphorus, potassium, selenium, and zinc.
- Amino acids: All 18 known amino acids.
- Fat: .16 gm in each and every orange!

Orange juice feasting can also be extended for longer periods if wished. Some I have read of go for 30 days, again under professional supervision. Now that you are ingesting a food source, it is vital to exercise – but do so with low intensity. Get outside and walk! [Being] active in the out-of-doors in the sun repleats your body with vita[min D,] negative ions, refreshes your being and aids in the detoxificatio[n] process. It also helps raise your metabolism. If you cannot do [a few] hours throughout your day, work up to it. Your body will love y[ou for] it!

The third part of this fasting/feasting journey is that of integrating fruit smoothies and green smoothies back into your d[iet.] This prepares your body for the final part of this experience - goi[ng] back onto solid foods. Smoothies are more dense than the orang[e] juice, however because they are pre-masticated in your blender, [they] are still easier for your body to digest than solid foods, allowing it [to] continue on its healing journey.   Breaking down the cell walls of t[he] greens is key for optimal absorption of their life-giving nutrients.

Research indicates that the nutrients in greens match all of [our] nutritional needs. Furthermore, greens are purported to help quel[l] cravings, and are nutrient dense providing high amounts of protei[n,] iron, and calcium as well as many other wonderful nutrients. Gree[n] smoothies increase HCL – hydrochloric acids are key in healthy digestion. Green smoothies will help get you back "online."

As with the orange juice feasting, you will need to continue t[o] exercise. You may even be able to increase your daily activity to a[ ] more beneficial standard.

Now I am going to share with you my diary of my own experiences on my cleanse experience!

Mattye's FRUGAL RAW Annual Cleanse 2008 Diary:

Everyone is different. The key to a successful cleansing peri[od] is to listen to your body. After you have transitioned into the cleanse your body will let you know when to begin incorporating solid foods again. You will begin to have cravings for solids after a period of satiation on only liquids. This will be how to know the time has come to end your cleanse.

This diary is the retelling of my own personal experience and is not intended as a set-in-stone day-to-day recommendation. While weight release is part of the experience, it is not intended to be a permanent effect. As you transition back to

30th Annual
Rio Grande Valley
Quilt Guild Show

"Stars Highlight
the 30s"

February 24 & 25, 2012

9 a.m.-5 p.m.

McAllen
Convention Center,
700 Convention Center Blvd.
Exhibit Hall B
McAllen, Texas
Ware Exit off Hwy. 83

Quality Vendors,
More Quilts,
Ample Parking.
Bigger and Better
than Ever!

Mark your calendar

More info:
www.rgvqg.com

solid foods, some weight will return and you will stabilize. I have included my release amounts only as reference points.

DAY 1: Water-only fasting ~ I am full of energy today! Very little detox happening at all just yet as my body processes its final remnants of food fuels. Today I did my usual workout of Army PT, a belly dance lesson, and 3 miles of power walking. I have had some hunger pangs, but quelled them quickly by drinking more water.

DAY 2: Water-only fasting ~ I am a little lower on energy today, so I am listening to my body. My only exercise was my belly dance lesson. Detox is beginning to happen. I woke up with a swollen face and have been having some mild headache pangs. My tongue is an icky shade of grey with a white coating.

DAY 3: Water-only fasting ~ Very low energy today. Stayed in bed most of it reading. No workout today. Not so much of those headache pangs today, tongue color is improving, but the coating is thickening. Still having some mild hunger pangs. Feeling very ethereal. I've begun having a strange irregularly patterned twitch in my face just below my left lower lip. It doesn't hurt – just an odd muscle twitch. Total pounds released in 3 days: 10.6. – I am at 198.2.

DAY 4: Orange Juice Feasting ~ I went into the o.j. feasting this morning around 9 a.m. I nursed 24 ounces of my diluted golden elixir until 1:00 p.m. I took alternate sips of water as I sipped my o.j. I wasn't hungry tonight, so I stuck to water. Total oranges consumed today: 2. I was higher energy today! I went outside and gathered up all of the black walnuts from the ground in my backyard and carried them across the street for a recurrent squirrel. I also did some walking today. Altogether, I spent 2 hours outside in the sun – it was rejuvenating! Beginning weight this morning: 194.6 – an additional 3.6 lb release!

DAY 5: Orange Juice Feasting ~ Today I had 2 of those 24 ounce glasses of o.j. Total oranges consumed today: 4. I didn't drink as much water as I am used to as I was out of the house all afternoon. I went to Jonesborough, TN with my Aunt and we walked all over that little historic town! I was bushed by the end of it all, but I'd spent better than 3 hours outside in the fresh air, walking and enjoying the day! I have been working on a very important bit of psychological healing and prayed for help in resolving this issue.

DAY 6: Orange Juice Feasting ~ Somewhere in the night, my prayer was answered! I now have resolution and forgiveness of all involved. I love how fasts make one's heart and mind so much clearer, so that you can focus on what needs to be shorn away! This morning I am not hungry – at ALL. I'm beginning my day with water only. Sleep last night was the most restful I've had in a long time. My tongue is still coated, and that healthy color underneath is darkening. I finally made myself some juice around 2:00 p.m. – I guess 4 oranges yesterday was a bit much for right now. I am nursing this 24 ounce glass (2 oranges), and will finish my day with water-only. No outdoor activities today – it is wet, rainy, cold, and very windy! I am in Art mode today and hope to knock out at least a 3 mile indoor power walk this afternoon. Well I got so wrapt up in art that I didn't do any exercise today. I am having to get up in the night to clean my tongue – perhaps this sudden sendentariness has to do with that.

DAY 7: Orange Juice Feasting ~ Well no sooner than I had resolution on the first issue, than did 2 more present themselves! I am beginning to feel that this experience is much like the case of Binkley in the old Bloom County comix who had an "Anxiety Closet" – where these big fluffy monsters lived and would creep out in the night to hang out with Binkley. My lips are beginning to peel. Today I have had 3 oranges made into my juice. It seems to feel like the right amount for now. I have also been constipated off and on, so I am taking a medicinal herbal tea that includes senna leaves to see if I can get things moving. I've been painting all day again. I think this is going to turn out being one of my better works!

DAY 8: Orange Juice Feasting ~ The medicinal tea helped, but I am drinking another cup this morning, as my tongue was even more coated than normal and I woke up with the taste of seasoned pork chops in my mouth!?!!? I've been vegetarian since 2004!! What gives??? Whatever is latent in my body from my meat eating days I want OUT! So glad I am doing this cleanse. Three oranges yesterday was right on par for what my body needed. I'll be having the first round of 2 after my tea this morning. I ended the day with 1 orange juiced up, so a total of three also today. I am feeling a little bit hungry still, but going to wait until tomorrow to boost my intake to 4 per day. I think that it would have been best for me to stick with only 2 the first 2 days, then three for a few days, then four, then more if I want them as I progress.

DAY 9: Orange Juice Feasting ~ Today I am not only going to have 4 oranges, I am also going to get in at least one power walk! I am feeling GREAT! My current painting is almost complete, and I have another in the back of my mind vying for attention – hopefully by this afternoon I can/will start that one! My tongue remains coated, but thankfully, no pork chop breath this morning!! I just noticed something occurring – my physical scars are fading – all of them! I have one on my thumb from this past year (food processor blade cleaning incident), and my c-section and tubal reversal scars, as well as ones I got when I was a kid! I can only imagine what this is doing for my healing on the INSIDE of my body!!!!!! Got some upsetting news this afternoon – my husband is in boot camp and got hurt – It may be bad enough that they boot him out, but we aren't telling family until we know the extent of his injury and what that means for him. He was crying on the phone, and I cried for him and his pain when we got off the call. But I never ONCE thought about food. I was in go-mode, doing everything I could for him long distance, and never once did I even think about breaking this fast. I did have a total of 4 oranges today and that was the right amount for me at this point. I also got in 2.5 miles of power-walking before that phone call.

DAY 10: Orange Juice Feasting ~ I am very tired this morning due to the outpouring of energy on my husband's behalf. More thick yucky coating on my tongue, which had me brushing my mouth and scraping my tongue in the early wee hours again. It's just past 10:00 a.m. and I am about to go vita-mix up my first 2 oranges of the day. I'm holding up okay from yesterday's news – in a mellow state of limbo. I am feeling fairly low-energy this morning – painting and if I am up for it, a walk outside. It's a beautiful day out there! OKAY – DID THAT EVER CHANGE! At 1:00 p.m., I was so tired, I laid down for about ½ an hour. Thirty minutes later I was outside not only walking, but mowing my lawn! I got ¼ of the acre I live on mowed! WOW. I had 4 oranges vita-mixed and LOTS of water today.

DAY 11: Orange Juice Feasting ~ I'm feeling well rested this morning, about to have my first o.j. (2 oranges). I've been having leg cramps at night – down the front of my shin and through my feet and ankles for 3 nights in a row. I also had something jolt around my left torso last night – it felt like lightening! Hurt too! It lasted only a second and then it was gone. Odd. I noticed this afternoon that I was having a minor break out on my forehead. I haven't had a bm in 2 days, so had a cup of the medicinal tea this afternoon to keep things moving. I think I brushed my teeth 3 times today! UGH – I'll be glad when this tongue thing goes away! It turned out to be relatively stressful day, but again, I never once thought of scrapping the fast!

DAY 12: Orange Juice Feasting ~ Well, when I woke up this morning, bowels were moving and my breakout had stopped and has almost gone completely away – only 3 pimples remain. I was having some cramping, as I am within days of my next cycle. Also feeling a bit bloated, but I am sure it is due to that. No leg cramping last night! YAY!! I did, however, have a fair amount of mucus and one sneezing spell in the middle of the night. Total oranges vita-mixed today: 5.

DAY 13: Orange Juice Feasting ~ Today I am exhausted – I didn't sleep well last night – the pets were too restless. The coating on my tongue is finally and thankfully subsiding! It's in an interesting pattern, too – only the right half of it has the coating – the left is clean and clear! I spent some time outdoors today, cleaning out my flowerbeds – I have lots of planting to do tomorrow morning. Some are bulbs, and some are seeds – quite a bit to do! Total oranges vita-mixed today: 5.

DAY 14: Orange Juice Feasting ~ Today I am upping my intake to 6 oranges vita-mixed. It's working very well with my body to just add one a day more every few days. The last of the pimples look like they are abating☺. Tongue coating is the same as yesterday. I worked in my flowerbeds for much of the day – it was so grand being outside in the fresh air, working the soil! I'm hungry today, but the extra o.j. is helping that. I've now split it into three 24 oz glasses instead of two.

DAY 15: Orange Juice Feasting ~ Pretty much all that remains of the pimples is a bit of scabbing this morning. I finally had an unassisted bm this morning (no tea) – YAY! I expect this to continue to be the case now that my intake of oranges per day is going up, and later next week with the integration of green smoothies! Tongue is still only about half coated and is lessening. I'll be out doors working much of that day again today! Last night I dreamt that I ate not just solid food, but cooked food when I should have been sticking to this fast. NOT HAPPENING! This experience is too vital to screw it up. Sleep last night was heavy and after my first o.j., I'll be ready to go work on the herb garden and planting the sunflowers! Well I got the gardening done and also mowed another ¼ acre! I'm tired, and many of my muscles are talking to me, so a salt bath is in order this evening. Total oranges vita-mixed today: 6.

DAY 16: Orange Juice Feasting ~ Tongue coating is lessening, again had a natural bm and I started my cycle right on time this morning. I'm having some lovely cramps right now, some of which are bringing soft explicatives to my lips. I was hoping for a reprieve on those, but I guess when the body is in purge-mode, it's going to give it all its got! It's going to be raining this afternoon, so no outdoor work for me today. I've already done pretty much all of the housework and it isn't even noon. It may wind up being an Art day as I wait for my husband to call me and let me know his status. No word at all this week from him, but I have stayed on track, none-the-less. In the afternoon, when it looked like I would not be getting a call, I was beginning to have a meltdown. Then the phone rang! It was my husband and all is well. He sounded fantastic! His injury is minor and they're taking good care of him. I went to bed early – around 8:00 p.m., as I was having some really bad menstrual cramps, and was becoming nauseas from them. Only 4 oranges vita-mixed today.

DAY 17: Orange Juice Feasting ~ Feeling tired this morning as all of the stress washes away. Not only is my husband okay, but his first military paycheck kicked in today!!! All of my money woes are abated☺!!! It feels almost like a waterfall coming off my back. Still cramping this morning but not as badly as last night. My tongue coating is now only happening on the upper right quadrant. Hoping that will all be gone by Wednesday! Feeling a little head-achy again to day, and craving solid foods; also very sleepy, but it's raining out. Eliminations are now back on track. I had 6 oranges vita-mixed today.

DAY 18: Orange Juice Feasting ~ It's my last day of o.j., and I have to admit, I am officially burned out on o.j. as of today! LOL!! Total pounds released on o.j. fasting: 12.6!! Tongue coating is next to nil today. I have some jaw pain, tho – Like TMJ is kicking in again – hopefully that's the next repair in this process.

DAY 19: Smoothie/Green Smoothie Feasting ~ For my first smoothie, I kept it at simply blueberries, orange and mango – then – later in the day, I had my first green smoothie of papaya, banana, pineapple, lime, arugula – and I have SO much ENERGY!!! I turned 42 this morning, and I feel 23!! Life is GOOD! People are a-buzz saying I look more like 22 than 42. My final smoothie for the day was avocado, tomato, cilantro, romaine, lime, and a jalapeno! My-oh-my that was good!! I've been missing my peppers something fierce! No tummy troubles at all on the smoothies today, even as varied as they have been. My energy is increasing, and I will be much more active for the 2nd half of this month than I was the first – and I am READY for it!

DAY 20: Smoothie/Green Smoothie Feasting ~ This morning I started out with a smoothie of cherries, peaches, banana, and arugula.

It's good, and not sicky-sweet – the arugula makes for an interesting, almost peanutty undertone in the drink. I think I will try to do one with arugula, hemp, ginger, peppers and fruits – might come out somewhat Thai-like! The coating on my tongue is pretty much gone today. I still have amazing amounts of energy, and will be spending the afternoon outside gardening, mowing, etc. I got a lot of seeds planted today, but no mowing. I couldn't finish but half of my evening smoothie.

DAY 21: Smoothie/Green Smoothie Feasting ~ The green smoothies are definitely giving me more energy. I spent much of the early part of the day running errands, walked all over the mall, then came home and had the other half of last night's smoothie...my first for the day at around noon. I had an epiphany moment about that today – I've been taking in more smoothie than my body is ready for, and not getting enough water. I'm correcting that today. It is vital that water consumption is kept high regardless of how much "liquid" is involved in juices/smoothies. This evening's smoothie was very cheese pizza-like! 1 Avo, 2 handfuls of romaine blend, 2 Roma tomato, 3 sundried tomato halves, 1 small garlic clove, 2 tsp basil, crushed red pepper, 1.5 tbsp nutritional yeast, sea salt and pepper, with water to thin it. Very satisfying! What I am finding odd is that I am suddenly craving things I would not normally eat – chicken, bacon, pepperoni...meat. I've been happily vegetarian for almost 4 years! This could be part of more detoxing as my body rids itself of previous toxins. One good shift that occurred today was one towards a positive body image – I suddenly realized that I am no longer "fat" – I am overweight, but that translates in my looks as solid. I am only 45 pounds away from my initial target goal of 140 pounds. That's right around the corner for me and it feels incredible after having been so "fat" for so long! I watered my gardens in well and planted two bleeding hearts and one dill. The jaw pain I was having is lessening and the coating on my tongue is miniscule at this point.

DAY 22: Smoothie/Green Smoothie Feasting ~ Last night was a very emotional one for me. Everyday I notice some new nuance to this fasting experience. I'm allowing myself to feel. For too long I have shut that ability away for anyone but my husband. I am beginning to really let my passions rule me again rather than my head. It's another one of those onion layers that raw foods and the right guides will help you through. I have to "get there" in me before I can "get there" in others and find ways of helping them to heal. I still feel that I am taking in too much smoothies and not enough water, so I am again lessening the amount of smoothies for the day. I am feeling parched this morning, so the sea salt was probably not a good idea. I planted some more seeds and then I did a good workout this morning...the first non-gardening one since Wednesday when I switched to green smoothies. I went outside and did the recommended kettle bell exercises, and then came inside and did 3 miles of power walking! It felt good. It's going to be raining off and on today, and was raining when I decided to do my walk, hence the indoor workout. It is vital that you work out each day after you begin the green smoothie phase of this cleanse experience. You have to wake your metabolism back up before you begin integrating solid foods back into your lifestyle.

DAY 23: Transitioning back to Solid Foods ~ I'm craving solids. I want to masticate in the WORST ways! In fact, I am craving things I haven't eaten in YEARS and in some cases would never dream of eating! GACK!!!! It's time to end my cleanse...

I'll begin by having soft fruits – a pear sounds quite lovely. I prefer my fruits fresh and juicy as opposed to re-hydrated, and I've heard that soaked prunes are also a good idea when coming off of a cleanse or a juice feast. I however, am sticking to the fresh fruits I have available. Bananas, papaya, blueberries, peaches – may make some fruit pudding in my vitamix today, too – having it on a spoon as opposed to a glass is inviting! During my switch to green smoothies from the o.j. (as predicted) I have had some weight return – about 3 or 4 pounds thus far, but I expect it to be a bit more as I incorporate solid foods back into my daily routine. Still keeping up with my walking and feeling fine!

DAY 24: Transitioning back to Solid Foods ~ I'm fruited out – tonight I'll be having a salad; using baby greens and kale, such as I was using in my green smoothies. I'm craving raw corn chips and fresh spicy salsa...but it's a bit too soon for such things. I'm going to try to stave off that craving for a few more days. So far no digestive issues with my transition back to solids. I have no interest in nuts or seeds – they sound terribly heavy and dense. The key is in listening to one's body, and I am at this point being reasonable with mine. A raw soup will go nicely with my salad tonight!

DAY 25: Transitioning back to Solid Foods ~ Okay – I'm starting the raw corn chips in my dehydrator tonight – a spicy habanero recipe I came up with and I've been dying to try out! They will take a day or so to make, and I figure my body should be up for them by then. I have no desire to make anything in the vitamix this morning. I want everything today to be solid!!!   Sliced bananas with a raw chocolate sauce sprinkled with dry coconut for breakfast sounds deeelish! Lunch will be soft veggies rolled up in crunchy green leaves...may even make a salsa for that. Dinner turned out to be some wonderful raw ice cream! Yeah, I know – I used the vitamix...but it was ICE CREAM!!! I'm loving my raw life☺

****

Well the next day or so, the habanero corn chips were finally ready, and while yummy, probably were NOT the best idea so soon off of a cleanse. I also *maybe* used a few too many peppers;) I had a bit of tummy trouble from those. Definitely back to the drawing board on that combo...

Are there things I learned and things I would have done differently? Absolutely. I found that I was having some latent eating disorder issues (I was anorexic as a teen) while on this cleanse. Lovely demons in my closet I thought were long-gone peeked out a few times to let me know they were still there and I had to curb my pattern of wanting to be in control of my body instead of listening to it. This was my first extended cleanse and I think I should have worked up to it. My recommendation for those who also have a background of eating disorders would be to take it slow and above all else make an unbreakable pact with yourself to LISTEN TO YOUR BODY– and end any cleanse when it needs ending. Start with something like one day of water only, one day of o.j. and one to two days of green smoothies. Then build up from there, but at the first sign of forcing your body "to comply," you have to be in control of yourself enough to back off from the cleanse. Having a "buddy" can also be helpful in keeping this in check.

Also, the green smoothies a bit thick and heavy when I first transitioned from the o.j. Thinning them with more water might have been a good idea. I also felt that I wasn't drinking enough water by that point. Hydration is key. Oftentimes we think we're hungry when we're really becoming dehydrated. One discipline I try to maintain in my own life is to counter anything non-water I drink with an equal amount of plain ol' H2O. I find I have fewer aches and pains that way, boundless more energy, and just flat feel better!

Cleansing is a powerful, amazing process! I observed and experienced some very incredible things along the way and I look forward to incorporating this annual cleanse for the rest of my life. I will also be doing mini cleanses periodically...most likely on the quarters of and ending on the equinoxes and solstices each year. While I have yet to incorporate it as a discipline, I still like the Ayurvedic practice of water only fasting one day per week as well.

For me, this cleanse was a springboard that catapulted me into a professional field that I had previously only dreamed about! It's September now, and I've gone from waffling about wondering what I should do with my life, to jumping in and going through C.N.A. licensure, gaining employment and planning to finish not only my college education as an R.N. someday, but also will be adding Reiki to my repertoire later this month. I'm also looking into adding the required clock hours of massage school for my licensure to what I studied when I lived in Texas. Long story short – there is a difference of about 250 hours required between where I now live and what Texas required at the time I finished my schooling there. As a side note – my artistic ventures are also flowing full perk – to the point that I have numerous projects in the works in my off hours! I feel as if I am uncapped and FREE. Free to be who I have always wanted to be – and finally free to spread my wings and really fly for the first time ever☺ The highs are indescribable...there are no more limits. Just bliss!

FRUGAL RAW! Sprouting/Soaking Tips:

Sprouting is a very easy process, and does not require expensive sprouting contraptions. I use screen-type colanders for mine. The important things to remember are:

1) Keep them moist but not sitting in water.

2) Rinse 3-4 times per day as indicated.

3) Keep them covered with a paper towel or cheese cloth if you prefer.

4) Make sure they're getting air too!

5) Time Saver: Once sprouted or soaked, rinse one last time and dry - you can then place them in plastic baggies in your refrigerator for easy use in the next few days. I like to start them on my days off so I have access to them throughout the week.

6) Due to their natural toxins NEVER eat raw kidney beans or soya beans. I have purposefully left them OFF this list. They have a high fermentation rate.

FRUGAL RAW! Sprouting/Soaking Chart

Seeds	Dry Amt	Soak Time	Sprout Time	Yields	Helpful Hints
Alfalfa	3 T	5 hrs	4-5 days	4 cups	Place sprouts on a window sill for sunlight on the final day of growing. This will serve to better fortify and green the final product!
Broccoli	3 T	6 hrs	4-5 days	4 cups	ditto on the window sill action;)
Chia	3 T	5 hrs	4-5 days	4 cups	ditto on the window sill action;)
Clover	3 T	5 hrs	5 days	4 cups	ditto on the window sill action;)
Fenugreek	4 T	6 hrs	4-5 days	3 cups	Use when small sprouts - they become bitter as they grow longer.
Flax Seeds (whole)	1 cup	6 hrs	***	2 cups	No sprouting for these guys - soak them for making breads and crackers to get the maximum nutrition out of the whole seeds. DO NOT soak ground flax.
Millet	1 cup	5 hrs	12 hrs	3 cups	Sprouts are very small - great for use in salad!
Pumpkin Seeds	1 cup	6 hrs	1 day	2 cups	These can also be used post soaking without being sprouted.
Quinoa	1 cup	3 hrs	1-2 days	3 cups	Use for tabouleh or couscous recreations!
Radish	3 T	6 hrs	4-5 days	4 cups	ditto on the window sill action;)
Sesame Seeds	1 cup	4 hrs	1 day	1 cup	Use hulled if wanting actual sprouts. Otherwise soak and skip the spouting time.
Sunflower Seeds	1 cup	6 hrs	1 day	2 cups	Can be used without sprouting - just go with the soak time for cheeses, sauces, taco fillings and sweets!

Beans / Legumes	Dry Amt	Soak Time	Sprout Time	Yields	Helpful Hints
Adzuki Beans	1 cup	12 hours	2-3 days	2 cups	Look for only 1/4" to 1/2" tails. Rinse 3-4x per day.
Black Beans	1 cup	12 hours	2-3 days	2 cups	Look for only 1/4" to 1/2" tails. Rinse 3-4x per day.

Black-eyed Peas	1 cup	12 hours	2-3 days	2 cups	Look for only 1/4" to 1/2" tails. Rinse 3-4x per day.
Chick Peas (Garbanzos)	1 cup	12 hrs	3 days	4 cups	Rinse 3-4x per day; these mold easily so make SURE they are not sitting in water. If making a hummus, you can skip the sprouting time. Soak and place in your food processor and season them up!
Green Peas	1 cup	8 hrs	3 days	3 cups	Ready when the sprout is 2" long.
Lentils	3/4 cup	8 hrs	3 days	4 cups	Rinse 2-3x per day.
Mung Beans	1/3 cup	8 hrs	4-5 days	4 cups	Remove the hulls post sprouting by rinsing vigorusly.
Navy Beans	1 cup	12 hours	2-3 days	2 cups	Look for only 1/4" to 1/2" tails. Rinse 3-4x per day.
Pinto Beans	1 cup	12 hours	2-3 days	2 cups	Look for only 1/4" to 1/2" tails. Rinse 3-4x per day.

Grains	Dry Amt	Soak Time	Sprout Time	Yields	Helpful Hints
Amaranth	1 cup	3-4 hrs	1-2 days	3 cups	Rinse 3-4x per day.
Barley	1 cup	6 hrs	12-24 hrs	2 cups	Use hulled barley; rinse 3-4x per day.
Buckwheat	1 cup	6 hrs	1-2 days	2 cups	Use hulled buckwheat; rinse 3-4x per day.
Oats (unhulled)	1 cup	8-14 hrs	1-2 days	1.5 cups	good for making sprout milk when mixed with sprouted rice or growing into oat grass.
Rye Berries	1 cup	6 hrs	2-3 days	3 cups	Rinse 3-4x per day.
Spelt	1 cup	6 hrs	1-2 days	3 cups	Good substitute for commercial wheat; good for some who suffer from celiac and wheat intolerance. Rinse 3-4x per day.
Teff	1 cup	3 hrs	1-2 days	3 cups	Another good wheat substitute; aka lovegrass. Rinse 3-4x per day.
Wheat Berries (hard)	1 cup	8 hrs	2-3 days	3 cups	Use for producing wheat grass! Remember to rinse 3-4x per day.
Wheat Berries (soft)	1 cup	8 hrs	2-3 days	3 cups	Use to make your soft breads and crackers. Remember to rinse 3-4x per day.
Wild Rice	1 cup	12 hrs	2-3 days	3 cups	Wild rice is black, thin and about an inch long. Remember to rinse 3-4x per day.

Nuts & Dried Fruits	Dry Amt	Soak Time	Sprout Time	Approx Yields	Helpful Hints
Almonds	3 cups	24-48 hrs	***	4 cups	None of these require sprouting. Soaking makes them easier to digest, and produces a much creamier texture for the nuts than you would get as dry. Soaking dry fruits will help you stay hydrated as well as save your appliances when processing them in recipes!!
Walnuts	3 cups	6-8 hrs	***	4 cups	
Macadamias	3 cups	6-8 hrs	***	4 cups	
Cashews	3 cups	6-8 hrs	***	4 cups	
Pecans	3 cups	6-8 hrs	***	4 cups	
Apricots	3 cups	6-8 hrs	***	4 cups	
Dates	3 cups	6-8 hrs	***	4 cups	
Prunes	3 cups	6-8 hrs	***	4 cups	
Cherries	3 cups	6-8 hrs	***	4 cups	
Raisins	3 cups	6-8 hrs	***	4 cups	
Cranberries	3 cups	6-8 hrs	***	4 cups	
Peaches	3 cups	6-8 hrs	***	4 cups	
Figs	3 cups	6-8 hrs	***	4 cups	
Mango	3 cups	6-8 hrs	***	4 cups	
Papaya	3 cups	6-8 hrs	***	4 cups	
Pineapple	3 cups	6-8 hrs	***	4 cups	

FRUGAL RAW RECIPES!!!!!!!!

- Smoothies
- Soups
- Appetizers
- Salads/Salsas
- Dips/Cheezes/Pates
- Chips/Breads
- Entrees/Wraps
- Desserts/Sweets

SMOOTHIES

Mattye's Sweet Smoothies

I like to make enough to share! Standardly, I allow for 6 cups of smoothie for two people...

➢ Coconut Heaven: Flesh and water of 2 young coconuts, plus enough ice to bring the level up to 6 cups in a blender. Blend until smooth and creamy!

➢ Honey of a Peach: 6 peaches, honey to taste, ¼ c. water, plus enough ice to bring the level to 6 cups. Blend until smooth and serve!

➢ Bango: 3 bananas, 1 mango – peeled and pitted, ½ c. water plus ice to the 6 cup level. Blend until smooth and enjoy!

➢ Banco: 3 bananas, flesh and water of 1 young coconut, plus ice to the 6 cup level. Blend until smooth and wonderful!

➢ Bancowi: 2 bananas, flesh and water of 1 young coconut, 2 kiwi, 1 Tbsp raw honey or agave, plus ice to the 6 cup level. Blend well!

➢ Watermelonade: Watermelon chunks to 6 cups, fruit of 1 lemon (no skin, no seeds), add ice to 6 c. after first blending the fruits.

➢ Blackberry Melonade: Watermelon chunks to 5 cups, 1 c. blackberries, fruit of 1 lemon (no skin, no seeds), add ice to 6 c. after first blending the fruits. Enjoy!

➢ Pumpkin Pie: 1 small, young American Pie pumpkin (peeled, seeded, and cut into chunks, flesh and water of 1 young coconut, 2 Tbsp. raw honey or agave, 2 tsp pumpkin pie spice, and ice to the 6 cu level after the first blending. Creamy wonderful Autumnness!

Mattye's Green Smoothies

Ideally, a green smoothie consists of 60% fruit and 40% greens.

> ➢ Banana Blues: 2 bananas, 1 c. blueberries, 1 orange (peeled and seeded), 1-2 handfuls of baby spinach (stems removed), and ice to the 6 cup level. Blend and serve!

> ➢ Razzaban: 2 bananas, 1 c. raspberries, 1 lime (peeled and seeded), 1-2 handfuls of baby spinach (stems removed), and ice to the 6 cup level. Blend and love!

> ➢ Strawbanade: 2 bananas, 1 c. strawberries, 1 lemon (peeled and seeded), 1-2 handfuls of baby spinach (stems removed), and ice to the 6 cup level. Blend and enjoy!

> ➢ Strawbawi: 1 banana, 1 c. strawberries, 2 kiwi, 1 lemon (peeled and seeded), 1-2 handfuls of baby spinach (stems removed), and ice to the 6 cup level. Blend and savor!

> ➢ Banpinego: 2 bananas, ½ c. pineapple, 1 c. mango, 1 lime (peeled and seeded), 1-2 handfuls of baby spinach (stems removed), and ice to the 6 cup level. Blend the decadence!

> ➢ Waldorf: 2 bananas, 1 apple (cored and cubed), ½ c. soaked almonds, 1 Tbsp. raw honey or agave, 1 c. chopped celery, and ice to the 6 cup level. Blend and serve!

> ➢ Peary Kale: 4 pears (cored), 1 lemon (peeled and seeded), 1-2 handfuls of kale, de-ribbed, and ice to the 6 cup level. Blend and enjoy!

> ➢ Peachy Kale: 4 peaches (pit removed), 1 Tbsp raw honey or agave, 1 lemon (peeled and seeded), 1-2 handfuls of kale, de-ribbed, and ice to the 6 cup level. Blend and savor!

Mattye's Savory Smoothies

For those who like it hot and sassy!

- Bananabero: 6 bananas, ¼ - ½ fresh habanero pepper, and add water and ice to 6 cups in the blender. Blend and enjoy the burn!

- Banger: 6 bananas, 1" – 2" piece of fresh ginger, peeled and grated, and add water and ice to 6 cups in the blender. Blend and enjoy!

- Kale Melange: 1 handful kale, ribs removed, 2 tomatoes, 1 parsnip, ½ bell pepper, ½ cucumber (peeled), 1 leek (white part only), dash sea salt, cracked black pepper, and water/ice to desired consistency.

- Borscht: 1 handful beet greens, ribs removed, 1 orange (peeled and seeded), 3 beets, peeled and cubed, 1" piece fresh ginger, peeled and grated, 1 Tbsp honey, and water/ice to desired consistency. This is a wonderful wintertime treat!

- Salsa: 2-3 tomatoes, ¼ onion, 1-2 Tbsp cilantro, ¼ jalapeno, 1 lemon or lime (peeled and seeded), 5 -10 oil cured olives, and water/ice to desired consistency. Sassy!

- Italiano: 3-4 Roma tomatoes, ¼ onion, 1 clove garlic, 1 handful spinach (stems removed), 1-2 Tbsp fresh basil (stems removed), ½-1Tbsp fresh oregano, sea salt, cracked black pepper, & crushed red pepper to taste and water/ice to desired consistency. Mangia!

- Mexicorn: 2 tomatoes, 1 avocado, ¼ onion, ¼ - ½ chili pepper, ½ c. corn, and water/ice to desired consistency. Add sea salt and cracked black pepper to taste. Ole!

- Chai Spiced: 2 c. butternut squash (peeled, seeded, and cubed), ½ c. soaked cashews, then grind/blend in a spice or coffee grinder: ½ tsp allspice, 1/8 tsp black pepper, ½ tsp cardamom, ¼ tsp cinnamon, 1/8 tsp cloves, ¼ tsp coriander, ½ tsp ginger, 1/8 tsp mace, 1/8 tsp nutmeg, 1 star anise pod, 1/8 tsp fennel, and ½ bay leaf. Add water/ice to desired consistency.

- Thai Dream: Flesh of 1 young coconut, ¼ - ½ c. coconut water, 1 carrot, 1 handful of spinach, 1 tbsp chopped basil, ¼ tsp. crushed red pepper, ½ c. soaked almonds or cashews, ½ tsp powered lemongrass, and add water/ice to desired consistency. Top with some chopped raw peanuts or cashews that have been lightly tossed with olive oil and sea salt.

- Curried and Green: 3 tomatoes, ¼ onion, ½ clove garlic, 1" piece of fresh ginger (peeled and grated), 1 handful of spinach, and ¼ c. sprouted garbanzos. In a spice/coffee grinder, grind ¼ tsp fenugreek, ½ tsp cumin, 1/8 tsp mustard seeds, ¼ tsp coriander, ½ tsp. cardamom, 1/8 tsp tumeric, 1/8 tsp crushed red chili pepper, and sea salt and cracked black pepper to taste. Add water/ice to desired consistency.

SOUPS

AvRAWgolemono Soup

This beautiful rich and creamy soup keeps well overnight. Perfect color and flavor the next day!

1/2 c. cashews - soaked for a few hours then drained

2 c. water

3 avocados

3 tbsp olive oil

1/2 c. lemon juice

zest of 1 lemon

1 tsp sea salt

1/2 tsp cracked black pepper

1 c. riced parsnips

1 tbsp fresh parsley - minced

Place cashews and water in blender - blend until smooth and milky. Add avocados, olive oil, lemon juice, zest, sea salt and cracked pepper. Blend until thick and creamy. Add a small amount of water and blend again if you desire a thinner soup.

Stir in 3/4 c. riced parsnips and parsley. Garnish bowls with remaining riced parsnips and additional parsley sprigs.

Creamy Carrot Ginger Soup

1 young coconut - flesh and water

6-7 carrots

1" pc ginger - peeled

juice of 1/2 lemon

2 tsp Braggs

1/4 tsp Oriental Five Spice Powder

Place coconut flesh, coconut water, ginger and lemon juice in belnder and blend until very smooth. Add carrots (grate first if using a standard blender), Braggs, and Five Spice powder and blend again until smooth. Serves 2.

Creamy Mushroom Soup

4 c. crimini mushrooms - sliced

1/3 c. olive oil

1/4 c. Braggs

1 young coconut - water and flesh

1 tsp grated fresh ginger

1/4 tsp cracked black pepper

Marinate the mushrooms in the olive oil and Braggs for at least 1 hour, then drain before use.

Place young coconut flesh, coconut water, ginger, and black pepper in blender and blend until very smooth. Add 2 c. of the marinated mushrooms and blend until thick and smooth. Add a small amount of water at this point to thin to desired consistency. (I like it thick)

Add 1 1/2 c. more of the mushrooms and do a light pulse chop with the blender to create mushroom pieces in the soup.

Pour into bowls and top with remaining mushroom slices as shown.

Creamy Tomato Soup

6 Roma tomatoes

1 avocado

1 celery rib

2 tbsp fresh basil - cut to chiffonade

juice of 1/2 a lemon

sea salt and coarse black pepper to taste

water to thin to desired consistency

Place all ingredients in a blender and mix until smooth and creamy.

Garnish with chopped tomatoes and a sprig of basil chiffonade.

Creamy Avo-Spinach Soup

3 Avocados

juice of 1/2 a lemon

1/2 clove of garlic

2 c. spinach, cut in chiffonade-style

1 TBSP olive oil

1/2 tsp sea salt

1/4 tsp coarse black pepper

1/8 tsp nutmeg

water to thin to desired consistency

Marinate spinach in olive oil, sea salt, pepper, and nutmeg for 1 hour.

Place avocados, lemon juice, and garlic in a blender and blend until smooth and creamy, adding water to desired soup consistency. Add marinated spinach and pulse blender to stir combine. Serve.

Can be garnished with additional chiffonade of spinach and finely diced fresh tomatoes.

APPETIZERS

Cheeze Sticks w/ Marinara Sauce

These are cream cheeze sticks coated in a more seasoned version of my raw parm then dehydrated for about 16 hours. First prepare the seasoned Raw Parm for coating:

1 c. dry sunflower seeds
1/4 c. nutritional yeast
1 1/2 tsp Italian seasoning
1/2 tsp cracked black pepper
1/2 tsp sea salt
1/4 tsp crushed red pepper

Grind sunflower seeds until fine. Add nutritional yeast and seasonings and blend until well combined. Set aside. This will make a full batch, and you will have lots left over.

Cheeze for sticks:
2 1/2 c. soaked sunflower seeds (drained)
1 1/2 tbsp white miso
juice of 1/2 lemon
4 tbsp olive oil
1/2 tsp sea salt

Process the soaked sunfower seeds for the cheeze sticks to a fine grind. Add miso, olive oil, lemon juice, and sea salt. Process until very smooth and creamy but also thick. The olive oil will emulsify the cheeze tighter the longer you process. Scoop into a bowl and set aside.

Spoon out some of the raw parm on a plate for coating the cheeze. Scoop a 2 tbsp ball of cream cheeze onto the raw parm and roll in parm until it is fully coated and you can form it into soft sticks. Place on sticks a mesh dehydrator screen. Repeat with the rest of the cheezes until all of the cream cheeze is used. Dehydrate at 105 degrees for 16 hours. The sticks should be solid and ready for dipping at this point.

Marinara Sauce: Prepare this sauce an hour or so before you want to serve.

2-3 Roma tomatoes
2-3 dried tomato halves - soaked
1/2 clove garlic
1 tsp Italian seasoning
1/8 tsp crushed red pepper (optional)
sea salt and black pepper to taste

Place Marinara ingredients in a food processor and process until smooth. Place in a bowl and cover with plastic wrap. Place in dehydrator to warm. Use for dipping the cheeze sticks!

Dolmas!

I wilted these in the dehydrator, BUT if prepared enough time ahead, the collards should wilt fine on their own - I'd prepare them in the morning and allow them to sit at room temp for the day if you don't have a dehydrator...

filling:
2 c. parsnips - riced
1 c. soaked sunflower seeds - coarse chopped
3/4 c. dried currants
2 tsp dried or 1 tbsp fresh mint
zest of 1 lemon
1/2 tsp sea salt

Combine all filling ingredients in a large bowl and set aside.
Use collard leaves for the dolmas wraps.

dip for leaves:
equal parts of lemon juice and olive oil on a deep plate

Prior to filling the leaves, bathe each side as you go in the olive oil and lemon juice mixture, coating each leaf well. Lay on a cutting board and fill with a couple of tables spoons of filling. Roll tightly and place on mesh dehydrator screen. Continue with the filling leaves until all filling is used. If desired/necessary, dehydrate at 110 degrees for 1 hour to speed up the wilting of the collard leaves.

Raw Falafel & Tzatziki Spread

Falafel

4 cups sprouted mixed garbanzo beans (tan, green, and black)

2 cups sunflower seeds – soaked

½ cup raw sesame seeds

¼ cup olive oil

2 cloves garlic

juice of 1 lemon

2 tsp sumac

2 tsp coriander

1 tsp cumin

2 tsp mint

2 tsp savory

cracked black pepper to taste

Braggs or sea salt to taste

Place all ingredients into food processor and process until all beans, nuts, and seeds are granular, but pack well. Adjust seasonings to taste. Form into ½" thick small rounds and place on mesh dehydrator screens. Dehydrate at 105 degrees for 8-10 hours or to desired doneness.

Tzatziki Spread

10 oz. tahini
½ lg cucumber, peeled
juice of 1 lemon
1 clove garlic
2 tsp mint
sea salt and cracked black pepper to taste

Place all ingredients in food processor and process until thick and white. Spread on bread for falafel sandwiches or smear straight on falafels.

Herbed Cheeze Stuffed Mushrooms

25-30 Italian crimini mushrooms - washed

1/2 c. garlicky cashew cheeze (see recipe in cheezes)

stems from the criminis

1/2 c. pecan meal

1 tbsp herbs du provence

1-2 tbsp olive oil

cracked black pepper to taste

Place the cheeze, stems from the creminis, pecans, herbs, oil, and black pepper in the food processor and process until very smooth. Use a piping gun to fill all of the mushroom caps. Grind fresh black pepper over tops before serving. WONDERFUL!

Nori Rolls

---NOTE: thinly sliced baby ginger can be soaked in apple cider vinegar with a shard of beet for a raw pickled ginger accompaniment!

Nut Pate (replaces the need for rice)
1 1/2-inch piece fresh ginger, peeled
1/2 clove garlic
sea salt to taste
1 cup cashews or sunflower seeds, ground
Juice of 1 lemon (optional - if you don't use lemon, increase the water by TBSP)
up to 1/4 cup filtered water to moisten

Process nuts in food processor until very finely chopped. Add remaining ingredients and process until smooth. This pate should be creamy, not stiff, chunky nor watery...spread down the length of raw nori sheets accompanied by these veggie combinations for fillings:

baby spinach leaves, grated carrot, green onions shafts, and mung bean sprouts or finely diced portabella mixed with 1 finely dices clove of garlic and sesame seeds or avocado, grated carrot, and green onion or cucumber or
grated beet, cucumber, and green onion or
diced broccoli, grated carrot and sesame seeds or
avocado, fresh asparagus, and grated carrot...

Place nori sheet on a dry surface, and fill on one side of the sheet, using the nut pate and any combination of veggies you like. Above are suggestions I have experienced, all are good!

CHEESES/PATES

Garlicky Cashew Cheeze

1 c. cashews - soaked over night, then drained

2-3 tbsp white miso

3 cloves garlic

juice of 1 lemon

salt & pepper to taste

Place all ingredients in a food processor and process until very smooth. Use to stuff peppers, celery, dip crudites, etc.

*variation - for a yellow, more savory cheeze, add 1 tbsp nutritional yeast to the recipe.

Can also be used with the "refried beans" shown below to make carrot chip nachos!

Raw "Refried Beans"

4 c. soaked sunflower seeds

1/2 cup olive oil

3 Tbls. tahini

1 tsp. sea salt

3 tsp. cumin

2 tsp. chili powder

1 Tbls. raw apple cider vinegar

Place everything in the food processor, and add a bit of water as you blend until it is smooth. The aroma is amazing, and is very reminiscient of refritos! You can also use this to stuff fresh jalapeno halves as shown above on the picture in Garlicky Cashew Cheeze –

Or to top salad:

Or make burritos!

Sunny Eggless Salad!

1 1/2 c. sunflower seeds - soaked

1 clove garlic

juice of 1/2 a lemon

1 tbsp apple cider vinegar

1 tsp tumeric

1 1/2 tsp black salt* (this gives it that egg flavor)

dash of dill, cayenne, and cracked black pepper to taste

water to thin to desired consistency.

place the first four ingredients into the food processor and begin to process. Slowly add water to desired consistency. Add spices and mix well.

serve with fresh tomato (shown above) or other fresh veggies, raw crackers or raw bread, or rolled up in collard veggie rolls!

*black salt can be found in most Indian stores, and can be ordered online. Also large health-minded stores like Whole Foods or Central Market may also carry it in their bulk salt areas. The name is somewhat misleading - while it is a type of salt, it is powdered rather than granular, and the color is actually pink! The flavor and smell is very reminiscent of hard boiled eggs.

Cashew Pate Stuffed Tomatoes

1 1/2 c. raw cashews

2 cloves garlic

2 tbsp lemon juice

1/3 c. water

1 tsp. nutmeg

1/2 tsp celtic sea salt

2 tbsp olive oil

1 bell pepper, finely diced

1/2 c. black olives minced (optional)

2 tbsp basil, minced

3 tbsp dill, minced

1 1/2 tbsp oregano, minced

1 1/2 c. spinach, shredded

2-3 sundried tomatoes, minced

6 large tomatoes, tops removed, hollowed.

In a food processor, process pine nuts, garlic, lemon, water, nutmeg, salt and oil. Place in a large bowl and gently mix in the bell pepper, black olives, basil, dill, oregano, sundried tomatoes, and spinach.

Scoop mixture into hollowed out tomatoes. Serve.

Raw Parm

1 1/2 c. raw sunflower seeds (not soaked)

3 tbsp. nutritional yeast

red pepper flakes, s&p to taste

Place sunny seeds into food processor and process to a fine meal. Add nutritional yeast and spices and process until well combined. Store in an airtight container in the refrigerator.

Sunny Cream Cheeze Spread!

2 cups soaked sunflower seeds - drained

3 tbsp olive oil

juice of 1/2 lemon

1 tbsp miso

sea salt to taste

Process sunflower seeds until finely ground. Add olive oil, lemon juice, and miso - process until very smooth and thick. Add sea salt to taste.

Sunny Garden Veggie Cream Cheeze Spread

2 c. soaked sunflower seeds - drained

3 tbsp olive oil

juice of 1/2 lemon

1 tbsp miso

1/2 c finely chopped combination of: carrot, celery, bell pepper, red onion, and garlic

sea salt & cracked black pepper to taste

Process the sunflower seeds in a food processor until finely ground. Add olive oil, lemon juice and miso. Process again until very smooth. Add veggies and pulse until well combined. Add sea salt and pepper to taste.

Sunny Green Chile Cream Cheeze Spread

2 c. soaked sunflower seeds - drained

3 tbsp olive oil

juice of 1/2 lemon

1 tbsp miso

2 anaheim peppers, dehydrated until softened then finely chopped

sea salt & cracked black pepper to taste

Process the sunflower seeds in a food processor until finely ground. Add olive oil, lemon juice and miso. Process again until very smooth. Add anaheims and pulse until well combined. Add sea salt and pepper to taste.

Sunny Flox (faux lox) Cream Cheeze Spread

2 c. soaked sunflower seeds - drained

3 tbsp olive oil

juice of 1/2 lemon

1 tbsp miso

1/3 red bell pepper - pureed

1/2 tsp smoked salt

1 tsp kelp powder

Process the sunflower seeds in a food processor until finely ground. Add olive oil, lemon juice and miso. Process again until very smooth. Add red bell pepper and pulse until well combined. Add smoked salt and kelp powder and blend until well combined.

Horseradish Pate

1 c. sunflower seeds, soaked overnight

2 tbsp prepared horseradish

1 tbsp white miso

1-2 tbsp olive oil

2-3 cloves garlic

2 tsp herbs du provence

salt and cracked pepper to taste

Place all ingredients in food processor and process until desired consistency. Serve with carrot chips, in vegirolls, etc.

CHIPS/BREADS

Sweet Bell Tortilla Chips

3 c. frozen white corn

1/2 c. white onion - diced

1/3 sweet green bell pepper

1/2 tsp sea salt

Place all ingredients in food processor and process until smooth.
Spread thinly on paraflexx sheets and dehydrate at 105 degrees for 24
hours. Break apart into chips and serve.

Olive Onion Tortilla Chips

3 c. frozen white corn

1/2 c. red onion - diced

10 oil cured black olives (make sure there are no pits)

1/4 tsp sea salt

Place all ingredients in food processor and process until smooth.
Spread thinly on paraflexx sheets and dehydrate at 105 degrees for 24
hours. Break apart into chips and serve.

Salsa Chips

3 c. frozen white corn

1 c. fresh tomato salsa

1/4 tsp salt

Place all ingredients in food processor and process until very smooth. Spread on a paraflexx sheet and dehydrate at 105 degrees for 24 hours. Break apart into chips when done.

Pizza Chips!

1 1/4 c. chopped onion

1 lg. clove garlic

1/4 red bell pepper

1/4 green bell pepper

4 Roma tomatoes

1 c. sliced mushrooms (white or crimini - not portabella)

2 tsp Italian seasoning

1/2 tsp sea salt

1/2 tsp black pepper

1 1/2 c. ground flax

1/2 c. pecan meal

Process veggies in food processor until pureed. Add seasonings, flax, and pecan meal. Mix until well combined. Spread evenly on 2 paraflexx sheets sprinkle with a light amount of additional Italian seasoning, salt and black pepper. Dehydrate at 105 degrees for 24 hours or until very thin and crisp.

Olive Bread

1 1/4 c. onion

3/4 c. flax seeds soaked in 3/4 c. water until all absorbed

2 c. sprouted buckwheat

1/3 c. oil cured olives

1 tbsp olive oil

1 tsp herbs du provence or italian seasoning

1/2 tsp sea salt

1 tsp raw honey or agave

Place onion in food processor and puree. Add flax seeds and process until white and gooey. Add remaining ingredients and process until well mixed and somewhat smooth.

Spread on paraflexx sheet and dehydrate at 105 degrees for 18-20 hours (flipping and removing the paraflexx halfway through) until bread is dry but still soft.

Pumpernickel Bread

5 c. sprouted rye berries

2 c. sunflower seeds

2 tbsp raw honey or raw agave

1 tbsp olive oil

3 tbsp raw carob or raw cacao powder

1 tbsp onion - minced

1 tsp sea salt

Process rye berries in a food processor until finely chopped. Add sunflower seeds and again finely chop. Add remaining ingredients and process until well combined.

Spread on a paraflexx sheet and dehydrate at 105 degrees for 18 - 20 hours until dry but still soft.

Soft Onion Herb Bread

2 c. sprouted buckwheat

¾ c. whole flax seeds, soaked in ¾ c. water until water is absorbed

1 small – medium onion – pureed.

½ c. olive oil

2 tsp. savory or herbs du provence

generous grinding of black pepper

½ tsp. sea salt

Puree onion and then add the flax seeds, olive oil, and herbs. Process until thick and white. Add buckwheat and process until well blended and groats are broken up. Spread on paraflex sheet and dehydrate at 105 degrees for 18- 20 hours, flipping and removing the paraflex sheet after 4 - 5 hours. Slice into desired sized slices and store in airtight containers in the refrigerator.

Soft Honey Wheat Bread

3 c. sprouted soft wheat berries

1 c. milled flax seed

1/4 c. raw honey

2-3 TBSP olive oil

Process in food processor until ground and well blended. Spread on paraflex sheet and dehydrate at 105 degrees for 4 - 5 hours then flip and carefully peel away the paraflex sheet. Allow to dehydrate for an additional 2 - 3 hours, until of desired doneness. Slice into desired sized slices and store in airtight containers in the refrigerator.

***This makes an EXCELLENT raw French toast! Simply sprinkle a bit of cinnamon on the desired number of previously made slices, and warm in the dehydrator. Serve with raw agave or honey and fresh fruits.

SALADS / SALSAS / CONDIMENTS

Greek Grapes and Cheeze Salad

This is a salad I used to make in my lacto-vegetarian days, and is a good one to do when you can get a good deal on fresh grapes. I have now Raw-a-tized it! You will need to make a recipe of the cheeze sticks (see below) and make them half sticks (elongated cubes)instead of whole ones...this is a salad to feed a big family!

1 head romaine lettuce
1 head red leaf lettuce
1 c. green grapes
1 c. black grapes

1 recipe cheeze sticks (start 16 hours ahead of when you want to make this salad so they're fresh and warm)

Lemon Vinaigrette Dressing:
1/2 c. olive oil
1/3 c. fresh lemon juice
1/4 tsp savory
1/4 tsp sea salt
1/4 tsp black pepper

Wash both heads of lettuce leaves and let dry. Break up into a large bowl. Add grapes. Prepare the dressing and mix well. When ready to serve this salad, toss the salad with the dressing, reserving a small amount for drizzle on individual salads after the salads have been plated and topped with the cheeze cubes. Serve.

Nacho Salad

1-2 c. romaine leaves

1 c. tomato salsa (recipe is in this section)

1/4 c. oil-cured black olives

Sunny Sour Cream (recipe is in this section)

Salsa Chips (recipe is in the chips/breads section) and/or

Olive Onion Tortilla Chips (recipe is in the chips/breads section)

Make a bed of the romaine on a plate and top with salsa and olives.

Add sunny sour cream and tortilla chips as shown...

Best Burger Salad

1-2 c. romaine leaves

1 med. fresh tomato

1 best burger patty (recipe is in the entrees section)

1 red onion slice - rings broken apart

1/4 c. raw pickle relish (Bubbie's or homemade)

Russian Dressing (recipe follows)

Sunny Sour Cream (recipe follows)

Place salad ingredients in a bowl and top with a generous dollop of raw Russian dressing and a spoonful of sunny sour cream. Add a generous grinding of black pepper.

Russian Dressing

1/2 c. Sunny Sour Cream (recipe below)

1 Roma tomato

1/2 c. raw pickle relish (Bubbies or homemade)

smoked salt to taste

Place sour cream and tomato into blender and blend until very smooth. Transfer to a bowl and stir in pickle relish. Season with smoked salt to taste.

Sunny Sour Cream

2 c. soaked sunflower seeds - drained

1 tbsp tahini

2 tbsp olive oil

1/2 c. lemon juice

sea salt to taste

Combine all ingredients in a blender and blend until very smooth. Chill until ready to use.

Coleslaw

4 to 5 cups green cabbage - shredded

1 medium bell pepper, finely diced

3 carrots, coarsely chopped

1/4 c. sweet onion minced

1/4 cup raw honey or agave

1/4 cup apple cider vinegar

1/2 c. raw mayo (recipe follows)

sea salt, paprika, and cracked black pepper to taste

In a large bowl, toss cabbage, green pepper, carrots, and onion. Cover and chill thoroughly. In a small bowl, combine honey or agave, apple cider vinegar, and raw mayo. Season to taste with sea salt, paprika, and pepper. Pour over vegetables and toss before serving.

Makes about 5 to 6 cups of coleslaw.

Raw Mayo

Blend in a blender until smooth:

1/2 c cashews, soaked overnight

1/4 cup water

juice of 1/2 a lemon

1/2 garlic clove

1/2 tsp salt

dash or two of paprika

Add in a steady stream, until mayo becomes emulsified:

1/2 to 1 c olive oil

Mustard "Potato" Salad

2 pounds jicama - peeled and cubed small

1 small red onion

1/4 c. tahini

1/2 tsp tumeric

1 tsp honey

1 tbsp apple cider vinegar

1/2 c. raw pickle relish (Bubbie's brand or homemade)

1/2 - 3/4 c. raw mayo

1/4 c. oil cured black olives - diced

1/4 tsp dill weed

1/2 tsp sea salt

1/4 tsp. black pepper

Place jicama, onion, pickle relish, and olives in a large bowl. Mix tahini, honey, tumeric, and vinegar until well combined. Add to jicama mix, along with raw mayo and seasonings. Stir until evenly coated and combined. Chill until serving.

Green Pea Salad

1 lb. fresh or frozen sweet green peas (thawed if frozen)

1/2 c. red bell pepper - diced finely

1/2 c. grated carrot

1/4 c. white onion - minced

1/4 c. raw pickle relish (Bubbie's brand is good if you don't make your own)

3/4 c. raw mayo

sea salt and cracked black pepper to taste

Place all ingredients in a large bowl and stir well. Serve chilled.

Carrot Raisin Slaw

4-5 carrots - grated

1/2 c. raisins

1/2 c. raw mayo (more if you like it wetter)

sea salt to taste

Place all ingredients in a bowl and stir well. Serve or chill until ready to serve.

Mediterranean Salad

3 c. spinach

1 thick slice onion, cut in half and separated

10 slices dried or dehydrated Roma tomatoes (soaked in olive oil to soften)

10 oil cured black olives

2 tbsp coarsely chopped macadamias

2-3 sprigs of dill weed - separated and broken small

2 tbsp dried bilberries or currants

zest of 1/2 lemon

juice of 1/2 lemon

1-2 tbsp olive oil

cracked pepper to taste (the olive and dried tomatoes add a bit of saltiness - taste before salting!

Toss all ingredients together until salad is well mixed and coated. Serve!

Creamy Spinach Salad

1/2 pound fresh spinach

2 avocados, cubed

1/2 red onion, sliced

1/2 lemon, juiced

1/4 tsp sea salt

Toss all ingredients by hand (literally) until avocado is partially smashed and forms a chunky dressing. Serve! YUM!!!

Habanero Solar Salsa (topping a salad)

1 clove garlic

1 medium jalapeno pepper (with seeds)

1/2 habanero pepper (with seeds)

1/2 large purple onion

1 pink tomato

1 yellow tomato

1 orange, peeled and seeded

1/3 bunch cilantro

sea salt and pepper to taste

Begin by placing the garlic, jalapeno, habanero and onion in the food processor. Pulse until all is finely chopped. Remove from processor and set into a large bowl. Set aside. Process the tomatoes until diced, and add to the onion/pepper mixture. Process the orange and cilantro similarly, and add to the salsa mixture. Stir well and season with salt and pepper to taste.

Pineapple Mango Salsa

1 c. fresh pineapple - diced
1 mango - diced
1/4 c. red onion - finely diced
1/4 c. cilantro - minced
1/4 jalapeno finely diced
juice of 1/2 lime
sea salt to taste

Hand chop or lightly pulse chop in a food processor the pineapple, mango, onion, cilantro, and jalapeno. Add lime juice and salt, stir or pulse to combine.

Pico de Gallo

3-4 medium tomatoes - seeded and chopped
1/2 c. onion - diced
1/4 jalapeno - minced
1/4 c. cilantro - chopped
juice of 1/2 lime
sea salt and coarse black pepper to taste

Hand chop tomatoes, onion, jalapeno, and cilantro. Place in serving bowl. Add lime juice and salt & pepper. Stir well to combine. Serve.

Guacamole - (an old family recipe)

2 avocados

1 Roma tomato - chopped

1/2 c. onion - chopped

1/4 jalapeno pepper - diced

juice of 1/4 lemon or 1/2 lime

sea salt and coarse black pepper to taste

Mash avocados and add remaining ingredients. Mash and mix well. Serve.

Creamy Tomatillo Salsa

3 tomatillos

1/2 avocado

1/2 c. onion

1/4 jalapeno

juice of 1/2 lime

1 tbsp cilantro - minced

sea salt & coarse black pepper to taste

Place tomatillos in food processor and process until pureed. Add avocado and blend until smooth. Add onion and jalapeno and pulse chop to diced. Add lime juice, cilantro, and sea salt and pepper. Pulse chop to mix. Serve.

Tomatillo Salsa

3-4 tomatillos - pureed in a food processor

1/2 c. onion - finely pulse chopped

1/4 jalapeno - minced

juice of 1/2 lime

1 tbsp cilantro - finely chopped

sea salt and coarse black pepper to taste

Place tomatillos in food processor and process to puree. Add onion and jalapeno and pulse chop. Add remaining ingredients and pulse to blend. Serve.

Tomato Salsa

Place the following in a blender and blend until smooth for the "sauce" of the salsa:

2 roma tomatoes

2 dried tomato halves - soaked

Salsa:

3 -4 medium tomatoes, seeded and chopped

1/2 c. onion - diced

1/4 jalapeno - minced

juice of 1/4 of a lime

sea salt and coarse black pepper to taste

Hand chop the Salsa ingredients and place in a bowl. Add the salsa sauce and stir. Serve.

Cranberry Relish

This is a tart-sweet raw relish that I modified from a family recipe. The original recipe calls for 2 c. sugar, which I have replaced with 11 pitted medjool dates. It is best to make this a day before you will use it, to give the natural sugars a chance to release. If you still find it too tart for your liking, add a bit of raw agave nectar to taste...

1 16 oz. pkg. cranberries

1 large orange – seeded and unpeeled

2 apples, cored

1 lemon, seeded and unpeeled

11 pitted medjool dates

1 c. pecans, chopped

Process fruit in food processor. Process or finely chop dates. Add dates and nuts to fruit mixture. Blend and chill before serving.

Serving suggestions:

Make a batch of my garlicky cashew cheeze and serve with the cranberry relish on raw crackers or fill jalapenos with the cashew cheeze and top with the relish...

ENTREES/WRAPS

Caribbean Red "Bean" Salad Rolls

Chutney:

1 c. dried papaya - soaked

10 dates - soaked

1/4 - 1/2 habanero pepper

1/2 large white onion

juice of 1 lime

3 tbsp raw agave nectar

1/4 - 1/2 tsp smoked salt

1/4 tsp cracked black pepper

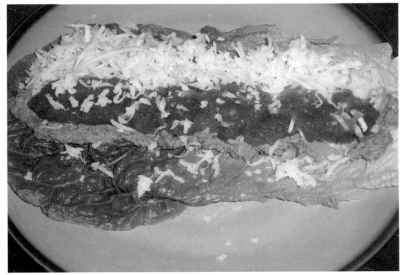

Place onion and habanero pepper in food processor and run until pureed. Add papaya and dates, reserving soak water. Process until it starts to become smooth (like an applesauceiness) and add remaining ingredients. Process to mix well. Place in bowl and set aside. Do not rinse food processor! Leave the residue in for the beans...

Caribbean Red "Beans"

3 c. sunflower seeds

1/2 large white onion

2 cloves garlic

3 tsp five spice powder

1/2 tsp. smoked salt

1/4 tsp cracked black pepper

1/4 tsp chili powder

1/8 tsp cayenne

up to 3/4 c. papaya/date soak water to desired consistency

Place onion and garlic in food processor blend until pureed. Add sunflower seeds and spices, and process until chopped. Add soak water 1/4 c. at a time to desired consistency. Spoon red "beans" into a bowl and set aside.

Roll up some beans and the chutney in your favorite lettuce leaves with shredded cabbage and dry coconut (shown) or make a salad out of it!

Green Enchiladas

I wanted to give those without dehydrators the ability to enjoy enchiladas...

tortillas:
collard greens - rib minimized

filling:
1 c. mushrooms - finely chopped
2 c. spinach - finely chopped
1/2 c. onion - minced
1/2 c. bell pepper (any color)- minced
1/4 c. oil cured black olives - chopped
1-2 tbsp olive oil
1 tsp cumin
1/2 tsp chile powder
1/2 tsp sea salt
1/4 tsp black pepper

Combine all filling ingredients and marinate for 1 hour. Spoon 2-3 tbsp filling (depending on the size of the leaf) down the length of the leaf and roll - these should be about the same size around as a regular enchilada. Place on a serving platter as you continue to roll more enchiladas.

Prepare the Creamy Tomatillo Salsa for topping and serve.

Green Avo Enchiladas

I wanted to give those without dehydrators the ability to enjoy enchiladas (revisited with a different twist)...

tortillas:
collard greens - rib minimized

filling:
4 avocados - mashed
1 recipe of pico de gallo

Spread each collard leaf with about 1-2 tbsp avocado (depending on the size of the leaf) and lay in a trail of pico de gallo on the avo and roll - these should be about the same size around as a regular enchilada. Place on a serving platter as you continue to roll more enchiladas.

Prepare an avocado sour cream sauce for topping:

1 avocado
1 c. sunny sour cream
water to thin
sea salt and black pepper to taste

Place avocado and sour cream in blender and blend until smooth. Slowly add water to thin to desired consistency. Season to taste.

To serve, plate enchiladas and spoon sauce over. Put remaining pico de gallo on the table and enjoy with carrot and or jicama chips...

4-Alarm BBQ'd Veggies

BBQ sauce (makes 2 1/2 cups):

2 medium tomatoes

8 dates – pitted

1/2 c. white onion

1/2 celery rib

2 cloves garlic

1/4 jalapeno pepper

2 tbsp raw honey or agave

2 tbsp olive oil

1 tsp apple cider vinegar

1/2 tsp tumeric

1/2 tsp smoked salt

1/4 tsp black pepper

1/8 – 1/4 tsp cayenne (optional)

Place all ingredients in a blender and blend until smooth. Cut up desired veggies in the following manner:

1) if using broccoli or cauliflower, slice the flowerets in half so you create a flat side on each).

2) Carrots, parsnips, or other root veggies should be cut to 1/4" thickness.

3) Pineapple, onions, squash, or peppers can be 1/4" to 1/2" slices or similarly sized chunks.

4) If using eggplant, slice to 1/4" and soak in sea salt water to remove bitterness.

Place cut veggies in a bowl and pour BBQ sauce over them. Stir well to coat. Let marinade for 2 hours before beginning to dehydrate. Set temperature for dehydration to 105 degrees and place marinated veggies on a mesh screened tray, sitting above a paraflexx covered tray to catch any drips that may occur. Dehydrate for 6-7 hours or until desired doneness.

Reserve any remaining BBQ sauce for basting about an hour before serving if desired.

Best Burgers

1 rib celery

1/2 medium white onion

7 oz. white stuffing mushrooms

1 cloves garlic

1/8 c. olive oil

1/8 c. water

1/2 c. cauliflower

4 c. sprouted lentils

1 1/2 c. sunflower seeds

1/2 c. nutritional yeast

2 tsp Braggs

2 tsp poultry seasoning

Process celery, onion, mushrooms, and garlic until pureed. Transfer to a bowl. Process olive oil, water, cauliflower, lentils, and sunflower seeds until finely chopped. Add to pureed ingredients. Stir in nutritional yeast, Braggs, and poultry seasoning. Mix well. Form into patties (I like square shapes for use on breads) and dehydrate on mesh trays for 10-12 hours. These stay moist when done due, so use a spatula to transfer them from the dehydrator mesh.

white corn tortilla:

4 c. frozen white corn

1/2 c. flax meal

1/2 c. lime juice

1/4 tsp sea salt

Process and spread evenly on one paraflexx sheet and dehydrate at 105 degrees for 3 hours. Flip tortilla and remove paraflexx sheet. Dehydrate an additional 2 hours. Then cut in half:

Spread with Sunny Green Chile Cream Cheeze and place slices of best burger in a double row down the length of the tortilla. Roll into two tight enchiladas:

Place back into the dehydrator for 1-2 hours or until ready to serve. Top with Chile Lime Sour Cream Sauce (recipe below) and a fresh tomato salsa (shown), tomatillo salsa or pico de gallo.

Chile Lime Sour Cream Sauce:

2 c. soaked sunflower seeds - drained
1 tbsp tahini
2 tbsp olive oil
1/2 c. lime juice
1 anaheim chile (previously dehydrated at 105 degrees for 6 hours to soften)
1/2 tsp sea salt
1/4 tsp black pepper
3/4 c. water to thin to desired consistency

Place all ingredients (except water) in a blender and blend until very smooth. Add water slowly until desired consistency for sauce is attained.

Avocado Enchiladas

white corn tortilla:

4 c. frozen white corn
1/2 c. flax meal
1/2 c. lime juice
1/4 tsp sea salt

Process and spread evenly on one paraflexx sheet and dehydrate at 105 degrees for 3 hours. Flip tortilla and remove paraflexx sheet. Dehydrate an additional 1-2 hours. Then cut in half.

filling:
3 avocados - cubed
1 recipe of pico de gallo (in the salads/salsas section)

Split the cubed avocados between the two tortillas (long ways) then add pico de gallo by the tablespoon down the length of the avocados. Roll up and place back on mesh sheet and dehydrate for an additonal 1-2 hours until ready to serve.

Prepare an avocado sour cream sauce for topping:

1 avocado
1 c. sunny sour cream
water to thin
sea salt and black pepper to taste

Place avocado and sour cream in blender and blend until smooth. Slowly add water to thin to desired consistency. Season to taste.

To serve, plate enchiladas and spoon sauce over. Put remaining pico de gallo on the table with raw corn chips of any variety!

Rueburger

This is a best burger sandwiched between two slices of the pumpernickel bread, dressed with raw Russian dressing on one slice, and sunny cream cheeze on the other, accompanied by a generous helping of Bubbie's Sauerkraut (yes, it's raw - or you can make your own).

LiveBurgers!

1 pound sunflower seeds (ground)

1 pound organic carrots (shredded)

1 onion (minced)

1 fajita bell pepper (minced)

2 tbsp fresh basil

1 tsp fresh sage

1 tbsp olive oil

1 tbsp raw honey or raw agave

2 tbsp Mrs. Dash (your choice of flavor)

3 tbsp nutritional yeast

1 tsp sea salt

Mix all ingredients in a large mixing bowl. Form into patties and plate with fresh sliced tomatoes, onion, raw pickles and the like!

Pickles

3 small-to-medium cucumbers sliced (you want smaller seeds)

raw apple cider vinegar

water

1/2 T Celtic Sea Salt

1 T black peppercorns

4 bay leaves

6 cloves garlic

3 dried chili pepper, whole

2 sprigs of fresh oregano

1 T fresh dill weed/flower

Slice the cucumbers to desired thickness and set aside. In a Quart sized mason jar, layer in all the spices and herbs, alternating packing in the slices cucumbers. Pour apple cider vinegar in the jar until 3/4 full. Fill remaining space in the jar with water. Tightly close the lid. Shake well and refrigerate for 1 week to pickle.

**I have also used this recipe to pickle green tomatoes!! YUMMMM!

Fyshburgers

fyshburger:

1 c. Liveburger (see recipe above pickles)
1/4 c. chopped raw pickles
1/2 sheet raw nori (cut into small pieces)
1 tsp. dill weed

mix together and set aside.

fysh sauce:

1 thick slice of white onion
2 tbsp tahini
1/4 c. olive oil
1 tsp. apple cider vinegar
1/2 tsp dill weed
1/2 tsp basil
sea salt & pepper to taste

place all in food processor and blend until tick and smooth. If mixture isn't creamy enough, add olive oil by the tablespoon until desired consistency is reached. Adjust seasoning to taste.

On a large plate, make a fish-shaped bed using the fysh sauce. Form the body of the fysh (pictured) and lay atop the fysh sauce. Use a small pumpkin seed, raisin, etc for the eye of the fysh, and a single salad leaf for the side fin.

Serve with a mixed green salad.

Poor Mattye's Raw Tacos

Due to a very limited budget and
an amazing hankering, I developed
a new raw taco recipe!

Sunflower Seeds are the most
cost-effective seed/nut you can buy,
so I used them as my base.

Give these sunny seed tacos a try –
they are REALLY good!

Filling:

1 1/2 c. raw sunflower seeds
juice of 1/2 a lime
1 medium onion
1 - 2 tbsp mexican chili powder (I like 2 tbsp, but that's me)
sea salt and pepper to taste

place all filling ingredients in the food processor and blend until you have a thick,
slightly chunky orange pate. Set in a bowl for serving.

shells = collard greens

toppings: romaine lettuce, diced tomatoes, diced onion, sliced jalapenos...and if you
really want to go all out, serve with guacamole, a salsa, and/or sunny sour cream!

Tandoori Marinade for Veggie Kabobs

For the veggie kabob part, use things such as: tomatoes, zucchini, peppers, onions, pineapple, mushrooms, yellow squash, cauliflower, broccoli. If using cruciferites, start them first in the dehydrator and add softer veggies to the skewers 2 hours before serving.

1/2 c. soaked cashews (drained)

3/4 c. water

1 medium onion

2 cloves garlic

1" pc. fresh ginger - peeled and grated

3 tbsp lemon juice

1 tbsp ground coriander

1 tsp ground cumin

1 tsp ground tumeric

1 tsp garam masala

1/4 tsp ground nutmeg

1/4 tsp ground cloves

1/4 tsp ground cinnamon

2 tbsp olive oil

1/2 tsp sea salt

1/4 tsp cracked black pepper

1/4 tsp. cayenne pepper

Marinate veggies of your choice for at least 2 hours. Reserve marinade for basting. Skewer and dehydrate harder veggies for 3 hours, basting once halfway through. At the end of 3 hours, add the softer veggies baste again and dehydrate for 2 additional hours. Baste a final time 1 hour before serving.

Serve with any combo of other raw Indian dishes, such as the saag paneer, riced pilaf, kofta curry or matar paneer.

Saag Paneer

1 pound spinach

2 tbsp olive oil

1/4 tsp. asafoetida (hing)

1/2 teaspoon freshly grated ginger

1/4 tsp red pepper flakes

2 tsp ground coriander

1 1/2 tsp ground cumin

1/4 tsp. star anise

1/2 tsp cinnamon

1/4 tsp cloves

1/4 tsp nutmeg

1/2 tsp tumeric

Marinate the spinach for 1 hour, then transfer to a paraflexx sheet and put in the dehydrator. Leave in the dehydrator for 1 hour to wilt the leaves.

Prepare the cashew cream using 1 c. soaked cashews plus enough water to raise the level of the contents in the blender to 2 cups and add:

1 tsp ground cardamom

Sea salt and cracked black pepper to taste

Remove spinach mixture from dehydrator and pulse chop to fine. In a large mixing bowl, combine chopped spinach with the cashew cream sauce. Plate, cover with plastic wrap and return to dehydrator for 1 more hour to warm thoroughly, or until ready to serve.

Serve over riced pilaf with mango chutney.

Mango Chutney

1 ripe mango, chopped
1/8 tsp sea salt
1 tbsp raw honey or raw agave

Slice mango over a cereal bowl, allowing it to drip into the bowl. Chop slices of mango and add to bowl. Stir in sea salt, let rest 5 minutes. Stir in honey or agave and serve.

Riced Pilaf

Cauliflower sometimes has a bitterness to it - if you prefer a sweeter rice, use parsnips instead!

1 head cauliflower OR 4-5 parsnips, peeled

1 lb. fresh or frozen green peas

olive oil to lightly coat

1 tsp ground cumin

½ tsp ground cinnamon

½ tsp ground cardamom

sea salt to taste

Rice cauliflower (or parsnips) in food processor and move to a shallow bowl. Add remaining ingredients and toss to lightly coat. Place mixture in dehydrator (covered) for 1 hour. Serve.

Kofta Curry

Kofta:

1 small cauliflower

1 c. white mushrooms

4 lg. carrots

1 c. cashews

2 tbsp. olive oil

1 tsp cumin

1 tsp coriander

1 tsp cardamom

½ tsp asafoetida (hing)

½ tsp cinnamon

¼ tsp. cloves

¼ tsp. nutmeg

generous grinding of black pepper

sea salt to taste

Place cauliflower florets in food processor and run until finely ground. Place in a large mixing bowl. Do the same with the mushrooms, carrot, and cashews individually and transfer to mixing bowl, making sure no large pieces remain. Add olive oil and all of the spices, and mix well. Form into ½" thick elliptical dumplings using about a golf-ball sized amount of mixture for each. Makes about 30 dumplings. Place on mesh screens and dehydrate at 105 degrees for 6-8 hours.

Curry sauce:

1 c. raw cashews

1 c. dried Roma tomatoes

1 c. water

****

8 medium-sized fresh tomatoes, chopped

2 tbsp olive oil

½ tsp dried chilies

1 tsp ground cumin

2 tsp freshly grated ginger

1 ½ tsp tumeric

sea salt to taste

Place cashews, dried Roma tomatoes, and water into blender to soak for 4 hours. At the end of the soaking period, puree until creamy. Add chopped tomatoes, oil, chilies, cumin, grated ginger, tumeric. Blend until smooth. Season with sea salt to taste. Place in custard bowls and cover with plastic wrap. Place in dehydrator to warm until ready to serve with the koftas. **NOTE: Wait to introduce the koftas to the sauce as you plate each dish.

Serve with mango chutney!

Matar Paneer

Matar Paneer is Peas and Cheeze cubes in a milk tomato curry sauce. Begin the dish early in the day for the cheese to have time to dry. If using frozen green peas, thaw to room temperature.

Cheeze Cubes:
2 cups soaked sunflower seeds - drained
3 tbsp olive oil
juice of 1/2 lemon
1 tbsp miso
sea salt to taste

Process sunflower seeds until finely ground. Add olive oil, lemon juice, and miso - process until very smooth and thick. Add sea salt to taste. Drop by tablespoonfuls onto a mesh screen and dehydrate at 105 degrees for 8 hours. Then using a spatula, turn each cheese cube and dry for 2 additional hours.

Tomato Curry Sauce:

1 c. soaked sunflower seeds

½ c. water

1 tbsp tahini

4 medium tomatoes - chopped

½ c. dried tomatoes (soak until soft if using a standard blender)

1 tsp asafetida (hing)

2 tsp ground ginger or 1" fresh ginger peeled and grated

2 tsp ground coriander

½ tsp tumeric

½ tsp sea salt

½ tsp ground cumin

¼ tsp crushed red chilies

Place sunflower seeds, water, and tahini in blender and blend until smooth. Add chopped tomatoes and blend until smooth. Add dried tomatoes and all of the seasonings. Blend until dried tomatoes are pureed and spices are well combined.

Place a 2-lb bag of thawed green peas (fresh if you have them) in a large bowl and pour the curry sauce over it. Stir well. Pour mixture into deep container that will fit in your dehydrator and evenly distribute the cheeze cubes, covering them with the sauce. Cover each container with plastic wrap and place in dehydrator at 105 degrees for an additional 1-2 hour or until ready to serve.

Serve atop a bed of riced parsnips.

Thai Green Curry Marinade for veggie bowls or Kabobs

For veggie kabobs, use things such as: tomatoes, zucchini, peppers, onions, pineapple, mushrooms, yellow squash, cauliflower, broccoli. If using cruciferites, start them first in the dehydrator and add softer veggies to the skewers 2 hours before serving.

Flesh and water of 1 young coconut
juice of 1 lime
zest of 1 lime
1/2" piece of ginger - peeled and grated
1-2 green Thai chiles
1 tsp fresh mint leaves - minced
2 tbsp fresh basil - chiffonade
1 1/2 tsp fresh cilantro

Blend flesh and water of young coconut until very smooth. Add lime juice, lime zest, ginger, and chiles - blend again until smooth. Fold in fresh herbs.

Marinate veggies of your choice for at least 2 hours. Reserve marinade for basting. Skewer and dehydrate harder veggies for 3 hours, basting once halfway through. At the end of 3 hours, add the softer veggies baste again and dehydrate for 2 additional hours. Baste a final time 1 hour before serving.

OR serve as marinated veggies without the dehydration process.

Serve alongside a bed of mung bean sprouts lightly seasoned with olive oil, lime juice, sea salt, and green onions.

Japanese Marinated Veggie Kabobs

For the veggie kabob part, use things such as: bok choy (bundled), tomatoes, zucchini, peppers, onions, snow peas, mushrooms, yellow squash, cauliflower, broccoli. If using cruciferites, start them first in the dehydrator and add softer veggies to the skewers 2 hours before serving.

2 tbsp olive oil
1 tbsp Braggs
1/2" peeled ginger - grated
1 tbsp sesame seeds
1/8 tsp wasabi powder

Marinate veggies of your choice for at least 2 hours. Reserve marinade for basting. Skewer and dehydrate harder veggies for 3 hours, basting once halfway through. At the end of 3 hours, add the softer veggies baste again and dehydrate for 2 additional hours. Baste a final time 1 hour before serving.

Serve with fresh mung bean sprouts tossed with a light coating of olive oil, rice vinegar, sea salt, green onions, and finely shredded raw nori.

Szechuan Marinated Veggie Kabobs

For the veggie kabob part, use things such as: tomatoes, zucchini, peppers, onions, pineapple, mushrooms, yellow squash, cauliflower, broccoli. If using cruciferites, start them first in the dehydrator and add softer veggies to the skewers 2 hours before serving.

2 tbsp olive oil
1 tbsp raw honey or raw agave
2 tbsp raw sesame seeds
1 tbsp Braggs
1/2 clove garlic
1/4 tsp dry mustard
1/4 - 1/2 tsp crushed red pepper

Marinate veggies of your choice for at least 2 hours. Reserve marinade for basting. Skewer and dehydrate harder veggies for 3 hours, basting once halfway through. At the end of 3 hours, add the softer veggies baste again and dehydrate for 2 additional hours. Baste a final time 1 hour before serving.

Serve with Confetti "Fried" Rice.

Confetti "Fried" Rice

4-5 parsnips - peeled & riced in a food processor
1 carrot - finely chopped
1/2 c. green peas (fresh or frozen - thawed)
1/4 c. chopped green onion tops
1/2 tsp grated ginger
1 tsp olive oil
1/2 tsp Braggs

Mix all ingredients in a large bowl until well coated. Serve at room temp or cover and warm in a dehydrator at 110 degrees for about an hour.

Rice Bowl with Orange Sauce!

Rice one whole cauliflower or 1 pound peeled parsnips and set aside (this is your rice).

Sauce:

One whole orange - peel and pith cut away and seeds removed

1 1/2 tsp chopped jalapeno

2-3 tbsp olive oil

2 tbsp raw sesame seeds

3 cloves garlic

1" piece of fresh ginger - peeled

3 - 4 tbsp Bragg's Liquid Aminos

5 tbsp raw honey or raw agave

1/4 tsp red pepper flakes

salt and fresh cracked pepper to taste

Place all sauce ingredients in a high powered blender. Blend on high until liquefied, yet thick.

Veggies: (any combination you wish): grated carrot, sliced mushrooms, finely chopped ancho chili pepper, finely chopped red bell pepper, snow peas - sliced in half, green onions - cut into 1" pieces, finely shredded kale or collards, etc. Mix sauce in a bowl with prepared veggies. Spoon up a bowl of the shredded cauliflower and top with sauced veggies - garnish with additional raw sesame seeds, chopped green onion, or peppers.

Can also be used to make Asian wraps!

Greek Marinated Veggie Kabobs

For the veggie kabob part, use things such as: tomatoes, zucchini, peppers, onions, olives, pineapple, mushrooms, yellow squash, cauliflower, broccoli. If using cruciferites, start them first in the dehydrator and add softer veggies to the skewers 2 hours before serving.

1/2 c. olive oil
1/4 c. lemon juice
zest of 1 lemon
1/2 tsp savory
sea salt and cracked black pepper to taste.

Marinate veggies of your choice for at least 2 hours. Reserve marinade for basting. Skewer and dehydrate harder veggies for 3 hours, basting once halfway through. At the end of 3 hours, add the softer veggies baste again and dehydrate for 2 additional hours. Baste a final time 1 hour before serving.

Serve with raw dolmas and Avrawgolemono soup (recipes in the appetizers and soups sections).

Texas BBQ Marinated Veggie Kabobs

For the veggie kabob part, use things such as: tomatoes, zucchini, peppers, onions, pineapple, mushrooms, yellow squash, cauliflower, broccoli. If using cruciferites, start them first in the dehydrator and add softer veggies to the skewers 2 hours before serving.

Texas BBQ marinade:

1 c. chopped Roma tomatoes

1/2 c. sundried tomatoes (soaked)

1/4 c. chopped red onion

1/2 clove garlic

1/4 jalapeno pepper

2 tbsp raw honey or raw agave

2 tbsp olive oil

1/2 tsp smoked salt

1/2 tsp cracked black pepper

1/8 tsp cayenne pepper

Place marinade ingredients in blender or food processor. Blend until smooth. Marinate veggies for at least 2 hours. Place on skewers before beginning to dehydrate at 110 degrees. Reserve marinade to baste. Skewer and dehydrate harder veggies first for 3 hours - basting once about halfway through. Add softer veggies and baste again. Dehydrate for 2 more hours, basting a final time about an hour into the final 2.

Serve with: Coleslaw, Mustard "Potato" salad, Green Pea salad, or Carrot Slaw.

Bruschetta Pasta

I have always done this recipe with how many people are being served at the time. I do NOT like refrigerated tomatoes, so I try to not have left over tomato stuff.

Pasta: Zucchini - 1 per person...peeled and julienned, spiral sliced, or grated in your food processor.

Bruschetta: (This will serve 2 or 3 people) You do NOT want to put this in the food processor. Do it all by hand with a good knife.

6 Roma tomatoes - chopped
6 - 8 Sun-dried tomato halves cut in small pieces (halves dried at home in your dehydrator is good too)
1 clove garlic - minced
2 tbsp fresh basil - cut to chiffonade
1 tbsp fresh oregano
enough olive oil to coat the mixture - but not sitting in oil.
sea salt and coarse black pepper to taste

Mix Bruschetta in a large bowl and allow to marinate for at least 30 minutes before serving. Give it a final stir before topping the individually plated pasta servings.

DESSERTS/ SWEETS

Lemon Tarts

crust:

3/4 c. pecans

6 deglet dates

2 tbsp raisins

1/2 c. dry coconut

process in food processor until dry
and well combined. The mixture
should be crumbly, but pressable.
Press into two small berry bowls.

filling:

flesh of 1 young coconut

1/4 c. coconut water

1-2 tbsp raw honey or raw agave

1 banana

1/2 lemon - peeled and seeded

1-2 tbsp lemon zest

Place coconut and 1/4 c. coconut water in a high powered blender* (let me know if
you use a standard blender and how it comes out) and blend until smooth. Add
banana, lemon, and zest and blend until thick and creamy. Pour into prepared crusts
and garnish with additional lemon zest and lemon rind curls.

Refrigerate for 2 hours to allow to set well before serving.

Serves 2.

Spiced Creamy Peach* Pie

*I have also done this with 6 Pears in the Wintertime instead of peaches, and it is equally yummy! I stacked it all into parfait glasses instead of making it into a pie, and garnished them with fresh pomegranate seeds and seasonal berries.

Filling:

First slice four fresh peaches (or pears) into a large bowl. Set aside.

Then blend up the spiced, creamy sauce:

2 peaches (or pears)

1 young coconut's flesh (no water)

dash of sea salt

1/4 tsp Nutmeg

1/4 tsp Cinnamon

1/8 tsp cloves

1 tsp olive oil

2 dates (pitted)

1 tbsp honey

Crust:

1 c. pecan meal

1 tbsp honey

1 dash of olive oil

3 dates (pitted)

1/2 tsp. cinnamon

1/4 tsp nutmeg

Blend well then pour into bowl and kneed with hands. Form into one crust in a pie plate, or leave crumbly to stack in parfait glasses.

Stir the sauce and the sliced fruit together and pour into crust or layer as parfaits. Garnish with mint leaves, pomegranate seeds, or seasonal berries if desired.

Serve immediately or refrigerate until ready to serve.

Triple Decker Brownies

This is a decadent brownie with a chocolate custard middle and a chocolate sauce drizzle/glaze:)

Brownie Base:

1 c. dates - pitting verified and soaked for at least 30 minutes

3 c. pecan meal

2/3 c. unsweetened cocoa powder, raw cacao, or raw carob

1 tsp. vanilla

3 tbsp water

Mix well in food processor until thick and well combined. Spread in the bottom of a pan. Set aside.

Chocolate Custard:

Flesh of 1 young coconut

1/3 c. coconut water

3 bananas

2 tbsp raw honey or raw agave

2 tbsp unsweetened cocoa powder, raw cacao, or raw carob

Blend young coconut and coconut water until smooth. Add bananas, honey and cocoa and blend until thick and creamy. Pour over brownie base.

Drizzle some of the following chocolate sauce over the custard layer and refrigerate until ready to serve:

Chocolate Sauce

While it is preferable to use raw carob or raw cacao, when they are not available or attainable, I use unsweetened cocoa and carob powders. Because this isn't an everyday occurrence, I don't worry over it...

2 tbsp cocoa, raw carob or raw cacao

2 tbsp raw honey or raw agave

1-2 tsp hot water (for dipping) OR

1 tsp melted coconut oil (- optional - if you want a coating that will harden when refrigerated)

Mix all ingredients in a bowl until well blended and smooth, adding the water only after you have blended the honey and cocoa well. You may decide that you like it as is! This can also be used for dipping fruits of your choice.

Peanut Butter

Shown here with cinnamon flax crisps. This peanut butter has a different flavor than the roasted variety that we all grew up with, but it's all peanut flavor!

1 1/2 c. raw peanuts (pre-blanched or shelled and dehydrated for 6 hours then cooled)
1 tbsp raw honey or raw agave
1/4 tsp sea salt

Place peanuts in a quality food processor (don't try this in one of those $20 models – I've burned one out trying before) and process until it becomes smooth and creamy. Add sea salt and honey. Adjust to taste if necessary.

Rawsome Chewy Caramels

2 c. raw cashews

18 dates - pitted

1 tsp. organic, alcohol-free vanilla extract

2 tsp. organic, alcohol-free maple extract

¼ tsp. salt

Grind cashews in food processor until powdered and natural oils make the nut meal begin to stick together. Add remaining ingredients and continue to process. If necessary, add up to 5 tsp water, 1 tsp at a time until to desired moistness.

Press into a small casserole dish, and mop away any residual oils on the top. Refrigerate for 2 hours before cutting to serve. Will keep up to 1 week in the refrigerator...if they last that long!!

Raw Donut Holes

(makes approx 17 holes)

1/2 c. sunflower seeds

1/4 c. cashews

3/4 c. dried coconut, unsweetened

1.5 c. pitted dates

1/5 c. dried pineapple

Place sunflower seeds and cashews in a food processor and process until texture is a slightly grainy meal. Set aside in a mixing bowl. Add coconut to the nut mixture and stir well. Place dates and pineapple in food processor and process until finely chopped and sticky. Add to nut/coconut mixture and knead well until you have a thick "dough" that can be rolled into balls. If too wet, add more dried coconut.

Roll into donut hole shapes and coat with additional dried coconut.

variation 1: add cacao to desired chocolatiness!

variation 2: reduce pineapple to 1/2 c. and add 1/2 c. grated, chopped carrots, 1/2 c. raisins, 1/4 c. chopped walnuts, and lemon and orange zest, cinnamon & nutmeg to taste.

Rhubarb Ice Cream

½ c. raw cashews soaked 10-12 hours, then drained

1 c. water

2 tbsp raw honey

2 sticks ripe rhubarb – cut into slices

1/8. c water

Raw honey to taste

Place cashews, water, and 2 tbsp honey into a high powered blender and blend well. Pour into an ice tray and freeze. Place rhubarb and 1/8 c. water into blender and pulverize. Add honey to the sweetness you prefer with rhubarb. Pour into a freezable container (like an ice tray or plastic baggie) and freeze. When you are ready to make the ice cream, gradually place cashew cream cubes and frozen rhubarb into the blender and blend on high until creamy. Serve immediately! This will make 2 large bowls, or enough for 4 to share.

Raw Any-Fruit Ice Cream

½ c. raw cashews soaked 10-12 hours, then drained

1 c. water

2 tbsp raw honey

1 banana - frozen

Fruit of your choice – cut into slices

1/8. c water (only necessary if using a non-juicy fruit)

Raw honey to taste

Place cashews, water, and 2 tbsp honey into a high powered blender and blend well. Pour into an ice tray and freeze. Place fruit and 1/8 c. water into blender and pulverize. Add honey to the sweetness you prefer with fruit. Pour into a freezable container (like an ice tray or plastic baggie) and freeze. When you are ready to make the ice cream, gradually place cashew cream cubes, frozen banana and frozen fruit into the blender and blend on high until creamy. Serve immediately! This will make 2 large bowls, or enough for 4 to share.

Banana Pudding

6 ripe bananas

flesh of one young coconut

1/4 c. honey

1 tbsp olive oil

5 deglet dates

nutmeg to taste

Place four bananas, young coconut flesh, honey, dates, and nutmeg into a high powered blender. Blend on high until smooth & creamy.

Slice remaining 2 bananas into a bowl, reserving a few slices for garnish. Pour pudding from the blender into the bowl, covering the bananas. Garnish with remaining bananas, mint leaves, and/or dried cherries. Place plastic wrap over the bowl and refrigerate for a couple of hours before serving.

Carrot Cake

Cake

1 c almonds (soaked)

¾ c dates (soaked)

3 carrots + 3/4 c. water pulped in a vitamix

1 1/2 grated carrots

1 T ginger

1 T orange zest

1 T lemon zest

2 t pumpkin pie spice

½ c raisins

½ c walnuts

2 c. dry shredded coconut

1 t lemon juice

First if you don't have carrot juice and pulp, juice the carrots and get that part ready. Next put the almonds and dates in a food processor and grind fine, until it forms a ball. Put it in a bowl with the carrot juice, carrot pulp, spices, zests, lemon juice and grated carrot. Stir until thoroughly mixed. Add the raisins and walnuts or coconut. This is your carrot cake. Form a circle or square or shape of choice on the plate.

Icing

3/4c cashews (soaked)

1/2 c. walnuts

4 dates (soaked)

1 orange (juiced)

1t orange zest

1-2T raw honey or agave syrup

1-2T lemon juice

Put all of these things in a food processor and blend until smooth and creamy. As for decoration use coconut, flowers, zest, spices you name it!